For Souls in Doubt

The Search for God, Love, and Purpose

Jeremy Kundert

Ember Petals Publishing

Contents

Acknowledgments

Thank you to Shad and Cynthia Sluiter for giving me the opportunity to devote a year to the study and writing of this book. Thank you to Jon Lai and Linda Hardie for the time and effort given in editing. And thank you to many others for the much help and encouragement all along the way.

.

Introduction

This book is not written for those with a general interest in matters concerning God, life, and the soul, but for those who are tormented by questions and uncertainties. This book is meant to deal with the deepest convictions of the soul and desires of the heart. Reading it will require striving of the mind, soul and conscience. It should not be read lightly or on a whim.

I suggest you begin by scanning the table of contents to see what questions each chapter addresses. Begin with the one you find most challenging or convicting. Begin with the one you cannot answer, the one you do not want to answer, or whose answer you believe you will disagree with most vehemently. Skip whatever questions do not piqué your interest.

In writing this book, I have come to a deeper, fuller understanding of the universe and the God who created it. It is my prayer that whether you are an atheist, agnostic, Muslim, Christian, Jew, Hindu or Buddhist, this book will take you one step closer to the truth and a relationship with God.

1   Is there a Creator?

Fundamentals of the Universe

The first law of thermodynamics states that
energy cannot be created or destroyed, which could
imply the universe has no beginning or origin. If energy
cannot be created or destroyed, then it must have always
existed. When a closed physical system undergoes a
process change, there is always the same amount of
energy at the end of the process as at the beginning of
the process and at any point during the process.
Regardless of processes, reactions, and energy-mass
conversions, the energy in that system always remains
constant. This is an important concept for the study
and application of many systems in science and
engineering. Anyone who discovers a method or
invents a machine that creates energy would become the
wealthiest person on earth. But the first law of
thermodynamics says that energy cannot be created or

destroyed. This leads to the conclusion that the physical universe is eternal.

The eternal, never-beginning physical universe of the first law of thermodynamics is conceivable and reasonable, but there is a major conflict with such a universe. Combined, the expansion of the physical universe, the second law of thermodynamics and the principles of equilibrium describe the point, manner, and state of the beginning of the universe. They leave no room for an eternal, never beginning physical universe. This apparent conflict between these competing laws of science arises due to a misunderstanding of the first law of thermodynamics. This apparent conflict will be resolved at the end of this chapter, but first Hubble's Law, the second law of thermodynamics, and the principles of equilibrium need to be explained.

The expansion of the universe can be seen by Hubble's Law, which describes the relationship between the relative velocity of objects and their distance from Earth. The further objects are from Earth, the faster they are moving. This indicates that as time progresses, everything spreads apart. When this observable trend of expansion is extrapolated into the past, all mass in the universe converges to a point in space and time in the past.

The second law of thermodynamics explains why idealistic, 100% efficient machines, systems, and beings do not exist. It explains why every process eventually stops. The second law of thermodynamics states that in a closed system energy flows from more useful forms to less useful forms. During this process, exergy is lost to irreversibilities (such as friction and unrestrained expansion). Exergy is the amount of energy usefulness a system possesses. In a closed system, while processes occur, energy decreases in usefulness (decreases in exergy) until it reaches a dead state where everything is in equilibrium and nothing changes. This is unavoidable because every system or process has irreversibility. A candle burning, gasoline combusting in an engine, an apple falling from a tree, and cellular respiration are all examples of irreversible processes.

The physical universe maintains the same amount of energy (as stated by the first law of thermodynamics), but it changes and moves towards equilibrium as it goes through irreversible processes. The physical universe continually decreases in exergy. The second law of thermodynamics shows how the physical universe looked in the past compared to how it looks today.

Equilibrium occurs when nothing in a system is changing. This can also be called steady state. When a system reaches equilibrium it will not leave equilibrium until some external agent or catalyst disrupts the system and unbalances the state of equilibrium. No process change can spontaneously occur, nor can the system unbalance itself. As long as the system remains closed, without the interference of an external agent, it will forever remain in equilibrium.

A closed system is a system in which no energy or matter enters or leaves. For example, the earth is not a closed system because energy enters system earth by means of sunlight and radiation. A sealed, opaque, insulated box containing an ant farm is a closed system. The physical universe is also a closed system because the physical universe includes all energy, matter, and space thus leaving nothing to flow in and allowing no room for anything to flow out. The only possibility for the physical universe to not be a closed system is if a nonphysical agent generated energy.

For example, two chemicals are poured into a beaker. Left alone they are in a closed system. They react with each other, undergoing a chemical reaction. This reaction continues until their closed system reaches equilibrium. Once equilibrium is reached, no further reaction or process can occur. It is impossible for the closed system to change once it is in equilibrium. However, if something is added to the beaker (making it no longer a closed system) further reaction may occur.

Here is a similar example. Two chemicals are poured into another beaker, but do not react at room temperature because they require a certain activation energy. Left alone they will remain in equilibrium, but as soon as heat is applied or a catalyst is added, they leave equilibrium and react with each other. They do not react until some matter or energy is added to their system.

Another example: examine a closed system of an apple at rest on a table. The apple and table are in equilibrium. Neither the table nor the apple can move. But if someone enters the closed system (making it no longer a closed system) and bumps the table, the apple rolls off the table and falls to the ground. There was potential for the process of falling to occur, but an outside influence had to break the equilibrium before the process would occur. It was impossible for the apple to fall until an external agent entered the system.

The Path of the Universe

There are three imaginable scenarios of what the universe looked like before the moment of the beginning of its current expansion. There could have been nothing. There could have been an eternal equilibrium of some energy complex physical form. Or there could have been a physical universe that experienced an eternal cycle of expansions and contractions. Figures 1-3 depict how these three scenarios would look. The diagram on the left of each figure depicts the general trend of the expansion of the universe and the diagram on the right depicts the general trend of the exergy of the universe as described by the second law of thermodynamics.

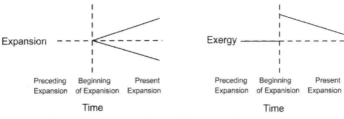
Figure 1: Coming from Nothing (Creation)

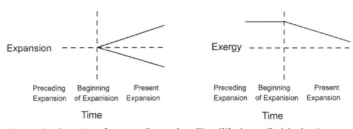
Figure 2: Coming from a Complex Equilibrium (Initiation)

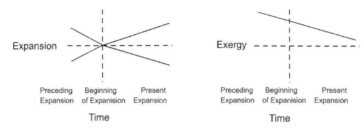

Figure 3: Eternal Cycle of Expansion and Contraction

Figure 1 depicts what the universe would look like if it was suddenly created out of nothing. As everything diverges from the point of creation into the present, exergy decreases. That means that the universe is closer to a state of equilibrium now than at the beginning of expansion. This is because exergy in a closed system always decreases. Figure 1 depicts the universe before the beginning of expansion as nothing. There was no matter, no energy and consequently no exergy. The universe before its beginning was in a state of equilibrium of nothing. Because of the principles of equilibrium and the second law of thermodynamics the universe could not pass unassisted from an equilibrium of nothing into an expanding, transient universe of something. For the physical universe to leave equilibrium, something must intervene from outside of the physical system. For the physical universe to increase in exergy, something must intervene from outside of the physical system. The scenario depicted in

Figure 1 requires that the universe have a beginning and that a nonphysical agent be the cause of its beginning.

In the scenario in Figure 1, when the nonphysical agent brings the universe from an equilibrium of nothing into a transient something, it performs an act of creation. Creation is more than the transfer of something from one physical system to another as with the addition of a chemical or heat to a chemistry beaker. It is the formation of mass, energy, or idea that did not previously exist.

Figure 2 depicts a universe similar to that in Figure 1, but instead of nothing existing before the expansion, there was something. That something existed at the point of highest exergy in the expansion of the universe. Before expansion and transience, the energy complex system existed in equilibrium. Nothing was changing; no irreversible processes were occurring; it was effectively frozen in time. For this second scenario to be possible, a complex system must exist in equilibrium. This condition engenders two questions: How did the complex system get there? Could it actually exist in equilibrium?

Those are interesting questions indeed, but there is third questions that must be investigated here: How does the equilibrium transform into a complex system in motion?

To bring any system out of equilibrium requires an external agent. How an external agent brings the universe out of equilibrium greatly impacts its future form. Interacting with a complex system with high energy potential is quite dangerous. Like smoking in a chemical factory or cutting random wires in an electrical substation, the potential for disaster is great. The manner in which the external agent interacts with the system will determine the trajectory of its future. With the example of the apple at rest on a table, how it is acted upon will determine its future. It could end up resting on the ground or flying through outer space, turned into applesauce or arranged in a bowl of fruit being painted by Van Gogh. The possibilities are endless, but the external agent will determine the future reality.

In acting upon the original universe, the nonphysical agent determined what the universe would become. Turning the initial state of the universe into a life supporting system rather than into a disaster would require an understanding of the constitution and laws of the physical universe. It would require understanding the effect of any disturbance or interaction with the system.

When a nonphysical agent interacts with the physical it does the equivalent of adding energy to the system and upsetting the equilibrium. In this scenario in

Figure 2, there may not be a complete creation of the physical, perhaps only a mini act of creation, and yet an act of creation none the less to send the physical universe on its journey through time. Indeed, there is very little difference between the first and second scenarios.

Figure 3 depicts a universe that contracts and expands without reaching equilibrium and always decreases in exergy. If this scenario is possible, then the universe could be in an eternal procession of expansions and contractions with no beginning and no end. Given that the universe in this scenario does not start in equilibrium, never reaches equilibrium and always decreases in exergy, it can exist and function without the influence of an external agent. It does not require a creator.

Given the condition of the universe today, the scenario depicted in Figure 3 is not an accurate trajectory of the physical universe. For the universe to pass through an infinite number of processes, it would need an infinite amount of exergy. A universe with an infinite amount of exergy (regardless of the number of processes it passes through) will always have an infinite amount of exergy. Infinite exergy would require infinite energy, which would require infinite space. Infinite space cannot go through cycles of expansion and contraction. The scenario of infinite expansions and contractions is not possible. The physical universe must have a beginning at which it passed from equilibrium to transience. An external nonphysical agent must have interacted with it to cause it to leave equilibrium.

The conclusion that the physical universe was created must be reconciled with the first law of thermodynamics. The first law of thermodynamics does not imply that energy is uncreatable, but that energy by itself is unable to create more energy. Whenever a closed physical system is observed, there is always the same amount of energy at the beginning of any process as at the end. The physical process will not create energy. For the physical universe to begin there must have been a nonphysical agent with the ability to create energy. The first law of thermodynamics does not limit the ability of an external nonphysical agent to create energy. It says nothing about the ability of anything nonphysical. It only says that the physical cannot create the physical. For the universe to exist, something other than matter, something other than energy, something nonphysical must exist.

The cause of the physical universe is a nonphysical agent to which many ascribe the name of God. When the word "God" is used, everyone thinks of the image of God they have been taught since childhood. For the purpose of this investigation of God and making an honest search for him, care should be

11

taken not to attribute to God any attribute or characteristic until there is evidence of such. It is difficult to let all the assumed attributes of God fade from the mind even for a moment, because most people have a defined image of a God whom they have grown to love, despise, or ignore. Overwriting that image is difficult. It is especially difficult for characteristics or attributes that are linked together in the mind. One attributed characteristic to God may bring another one along with it that does not belong to God. The reader must avoid the trap of assuming any attribute of God. A wrong understanding of God is far worse than admitting ignorance of God. At this point in this investigation, the following definition has been reached:

God – the nonphysical agent that created the physical universe.

2 Who created the universe?

The Uncaused Cause

Every debate about the beginning of the universe eventually finds its way to the idea of an uncaused cause, a being with no reason for existence, yet is the reason for the existence of everything else. An uncaused cause creates things, but is itself not created by anything. Every uncaused cause just was. At some point it existed without anything bringing it into existence. It may or may not have had a beginning, but exists without a reason or cause. Humans are rooted in the physical and educated in the school of logic. They struggle conceptualizing something without cause. This struggle is perhaps only matched by the human mind's struggle to comprehend infinity. Yet, because the universe exists, there must be either an uncaused cause or infinity or both.

An uncaused cause is similar to the concept of an origin. An origin is just the idea of being the starting point. Nothing comes before the origin. When applied to something like a person, it has the idea that that person does not have a creator. They are independent and do not need anything else to exist or survive. Independence and self-sustaining make them eternal. They also determine their own character and personality. Their desires, choices, and actions stem from themselves and are not determined by anything else. They are the sole origin of their own desires, choices and actions. In technical terms, an origin has independent constitution and master reference. Independent constitution means an origin can define its own character. Master reference means an origin can act, define, or create based on its own character.

Several other words are similar to the word "origin". They include person, agent, being, and soul. These words do not necessarily differ in the subject they describe, but in how they describe the subject. "Person" highlights the subject's distinct character. "Agent" emphasizes the subject's activity. "Being" focuses on the subject's existence. "Soul" underscores the subject's desires. "Origin" draws attention to the subject's independence.

Origins are the opposite of objects. An object is anything that has been created. A hammer is an object, for it has a definite creator. Fire is an object, for it stems from a cause. An idea is an object, for it is generated by a being. Objects are never independent. They are always created or caused by direct or indirect action of a being. Furthermore, objects follow the path of potential given to them by a person. A hammer never chooses to swing itself. It never jumps into the air and crashes down on a nail. Fire does not choose what it consumes or where it spreads. It is governed by the laws of chemistry to which it has been confined. An idea never produces anything until a soul creates something out of it. Consequently, objects do not take any responsibility for their actions. Everything they do has been programmed into them by an agent.

Origins have both responsibility and authority. When an origin acts, it does so because it chooses to. Because it has master reference (self-defined), an origin cannot attribute its attributes or constitution to anything else. When it chooses to act, it does so based on its own desire and preference with the understanding that it has the choice to act or not to act. The action of an independent origin is generated by the origin; thus the origin is responsible for the action. There is no excuse the origin can offer up other than to admit "I wanted to." The subject of responsibility becomes more complex as origins interact with each other, but the fundamental sense of responsibility for acting on one's own desires is always present. With responsibility there is also authority and ownership. An origin has possession of anything it independently creates. For example, when an origin produces an idea, no other origin can claim ownership of the idea. No other origin can insist that the idea be put into action or creation. The origin that produced the idea has authority over it and determines what will be done with it. It may forget it, act on it, give or sell it to someone else.

Randomness and Chance

Some may think the universe was not caused, but began randomly or by chance. Unfortunately for them, they misunderstand chance, randomness, and the physical universe. Chance is only a measurement of the probability that a given event will occur. Chance determines nothing. The probability of a six-sided die suggests that a five should turn up one time out of six rolls. The chances are one in six, but if a five turns up six times out of six, chance is not unsatisfied, defied, or broken. It is just that an unlikely event occurred. Chance is used for determining the likelihood of an event so people can act with better judgment. Some genius may determine the chance that the universe would be created, but chance did not dictate whether or not the universe would be created or how the universe was created. Chance requires potential. A six will never turn up unless someone rolls the dice. If there were no driving potential for the universe to come into existence, then the chances of it existing are zero. When someone says the universe was created by chance, they mean that it was possible for the universe to be created and that possibility became reality. But that reality is only possible through that external nonphysical agent.

Many people associate chance with randomness. When they state the universe began randomly, they actually mean that the universe began in some unexplainable, unpredictable, uninfluenced way. Randomness is the idea of something having no order or method of governance. When rolling a dice, it seems random which number turns up for each individual roll. But if the orientation, velocity, direction, spin, axis of rotation, material properties of the dice being thrown, and the hardness and geometry of the surface the dice was thrown onto were all measured, then the number to be rolled could be calculated. Saying a dice is random, admits inability to calculate the result of each roll. Saying the universe began randomly is just a confession of not knowing how it began. When science presents clear evidence that there had to be an external agent, it is illogical to claim creation occurred through randomness.

Requirements for Creation

The act of creation forms an object from nothing or transforms one object into a new object of different constitution and function. Creation of anything requires intent, potential, and conception. Intent is the purposeful desire to act, which implies will and preference. Potential is the ability to act. Conception is the resulting action and consequence when intent and potential meet. For God to create the universe he had to have intent and potential. These attributes of God imply that he is more than an influence or spiritual energy. He is a being. Beings have power and ability, desire and will, intelligence and imagination. Without any of these attributes, a being is unable to create. Without desire and will, the being's abilities lie dormant. Without intelligence and imagination, the being's desires never develop. Without power and desire, the being's ideas never become reality. Before time there was God and nothing physical. God decided to create the world. He imagined it and planned it. Then he acted. In acting he identified himself as a being.

With God as a being, he becomes much more understandable and less ambiguous, which bothers some people. They prefer God distant and fuzzy. When God is seen as a being, it becomes easy to see that he also has a defined character. People cannot define God whatever way they want. God is who he is and not who people might say he is. There is a defined God who created the universe and he does not conform to people's desires and imaginations. God has defined himself as who he wants to be. Like people, he makes his own decisions. He has the intelligence and imagination to make decisions, and he has the power and ability to act upon those decisions.

The fact that God is a being does not give weight or evidence to any religion or holy book. The focus of this investigation will remain on the physical universe and human experience; not on holy books, concerning which there is endless debate and confusion.

The Consortium of Gods

Was it just one God who created the universe? Or was it a consortium of Gods? How can people know which God to worship or serve, or if they should at all? This is similar to when someone starts a new job. They cannot know what to do until they know who their supervisor is, what his expectations are, and what the expectations of upper management are. If they understand the management structure, they can recognize to whom they are responsible and can determine how they should conduct themselves. By studying the possibilities of an independent God or consortium of Gods, it is not too difficult to see what people should do. If indeed there is a consortium of Gods, then there are three primary scenarios that need to be evaluated to determine how people should interact with the consortium as a whole and the Gods as individuals.

The first scenario presents the condition of two Gods with complementary objectives. These Gods work toward the same objective. They have the same goal in mind; so much so that, when seeking the same end, they follow the same path. The only time these two Gods with complementary objectives are distinguishable from each other is when they differ in roles. For example, if one plays the role of judge and the other plays the role of teacher, they are distinguishable. Although they have different roles, they work together for the same end. If one of these Gods desires human worship, then the other God will desire humans to worship the God who desires human worship. If both of the Gods desire human worship, then they do not fight for the worship of humans, but work together so that both are worshipped. Therefore, two equal, unified Gods are indistinguishable except in the roles they assign themselves. From the human perspective, there are not different Gods, but there are different responsibilities or dimensions of God. They can be understood and worshipped as one God.

The second scenario of multiple Gods is that of hierarchy. This scenario is similar to a governmental structure for the Gods; with one God reporting to a higher God who has more power and authority. If the highest, most powerful God is interested in the physical universe, then he determines everything in the universe and all other Gods are not Gods, but tools at his disposal. If the highest God ignores the work of the other Gods, then from the human perspective, he does not exist. Therefore again, the only God humans can know, need to know, or care to know is the highest God that is interested in the lives of humans. That is the God who created the physical universe.

The third and final scenario presents the condition of two Gods with opposing objectives. It is as if the Gods have entered the wrestling ring and are competing for a trophy. The trophy is the physical universe. The God who wins will take possession of the universe. If neither is stronger, then possession stays with whichever one created it in the first place. In this scenario, there is only one God that humans need worry about, the most powerful and interested God who maintains complete authority and influence over them. His authority is unchallenged, so humans need understand only him.

The conclusion of these three scenarios is that there is only one God that humans need to know. He created the physical universe and maintains possession of it through his power. There is no other God or being that is greater or has more authority or power than he. This God is under no obligation to anyone else. No one else can dictate what this God should do. It is his character, personality and desires which determine what God does.

3   Can we understand God?

Is God beyond our understanding? Is God understandable at all? Can we use reason or logic to study God? Much of what humans have learned has come from an application of logic. People make reasonable deductions from known facts and then test those deductions to validate them. Using logic accelerates learning and gives people greater depth of understanding of the world they live in. People can learn about God without logic, but logic will accelerate and deepen their study of him.

There are three static logic states in which God could possibly reside: logical, random, or illogical. There are also the modes of transience and steady state. Transience is change within or between logic states. Steady state occurs when the state is not changing. Humans are transient within their logical state. As their emotions, character, and understanding change, their interests, actions, and reactions vary. One day they may want to be a veterinarian for life and the next day an engineer. Because they are transient in character, the decisions and actions they make from day to day sometimes appear unpredictable. This unpredictable nature can make people difficult to understand. Transience requires routine testing to understand the current state. When routine testing is done, but no changes have occurred, then the subject is in steady state. When in an intimate relationship with someone, it is easy to see when something is bothering or unbalancing them. Their attitudes and behavior will change. They become transient. Regardless of what state God is in and whether or not he is transient, tests and experiments must be done to verify who God is.

The three static logic states are understandable in terms of systems of equations. Logical means that everything relates to everything else in one-to-one relationships and follows a defined, predictable pattern. In Figure 4, A=1, B=2, C=3, D=4, and E=5. Everyone can see that each number associates with one letter and each letter associates with one number and they follow a simple sequential pattern.

Figure 4: Logical State

Random means there is no predictable pattern, but the one-to-one relationships still remain.

Figure 5: Random State

Illogical means there is no set relationship between the numbers and the letters. The one-to-one relationships are broken. Some of the letters equal multiple numbers and some of them do not equal anything.

Figure 6: Illogical State

Logical State

The physical world lies in the logical state. Some argue that it is fundamentally in the random state, but everything ever measured follows some predictable logical pattern. Only those things that are beyond current scientific abilities are hypothesized to be random. In the physical universe, every system with a given set of inputs has a given set of outputs. For example, every time a marble is released at the top of a ramp, it will always have the same velocity at the bottom, provided each trial is conducted under the same conditions. While this is also true for a state of randomness, only in the logical state can the final velocity be scientifically calculated for any set of inputs. It is this predictability that enables humans to live productive, intelligent lives.

The logical universe is the result of God's desires and actions. Because God created a logical universe, he must at least be able to appreciate, understand, and interact with objects that reside in the logical state, if not also reside in the logical state himself. If God is logical, then his actions correlate directly with his character. Because of past interaction of God with the physical universe, the physical, logical universe is a window through which the constitution and character of God can be observed. It supplies a framework for interpreting the personal experiences an individual may have with God.

Random State

In the random state, one-to-one relationships have no correlation. There is no reason for why things line up as they do, they just do. Many people pretend they live in the random state. They know everything exists, but they do not care how it came to be. They have memorized how things work, but do not understand or see the relationship between inputs and outputs. They do what they want and do not consider the logical consequences. They live an existence of carelessness, thoughtlessness, and ignorance. Some people may think this is the ultimate utopia, but no one can live in such a state for long. Being thoughtless in a logical world frequently causes problems. And when bad things happen, people ask "Why me?" That question pulls them back into the reality of the logical world as they try to find a logical answer for their problems.

If God does reside in the random state, all is not lost. People can still learn about him, but they will be limited as to how much they can learn about him. Consider a child in school. She memorizes the names of different types of rocks. She memorizes their texture, pattern, and color. As far as she knows, the rocks randomly come that way. Whenever she sees a piece of granite or sandstone or marble, she knows what it is. She may value emeralds because they are pretty or granite because it is tough, but until logic becomes part of her rock study, she will never know how or why they developed. To study rocks in depth, she must understand how the rocks are formed and how they obtain their texture, pattern, and color. Once she applies logic to understand the many "how" and "why" questions, she can take her understanding and appreciation of rocks much further. She can make predictions about rocks and trust in the nature of the rocks. She can run experiments and perform calculations to determine which type of rock or how much rock she needs for a particular project. Humans interact with God in the same way. If God is random, people can memorize facts about God and learn about him through direct experience. But if God is logical, they can develop and deepen their understanding of him to a greater extent. They will be able to gain knowledge of him otherwise unattainable.

Illogical state

The final state is the illogical state. In this state, there are no guaranteed one-to-one relationships; there are no predictable patterns. Understanding the illogical state is difficult because people are so fixed in the logical state. Perhaps it would be fun to imagine living in this state for a day.

You pick up your red pen and write. The ink is both red and blue at the same time and place. And no, red and blue does not make purple; nothing makes purple. Purple never existed, even though you know what it looks like. The paper on which you are writing is not there, so you grab another sheet of paper that is both there and not there. Just to be sure, you grab another sheet that you know is there. You now have three pieces of paper, which is the same as four and zero. Your roommate yells at you for writing on the kitchen table with permanent marker.

Now it is time for lunch even though it is only 6pm. You just got up, but are still in bed. Actually you don't have a bed. For that matter, since being born at age fifty, you have never gotten out of bed. When you arrive at work, you realize there is no way you could be at work because you are still sleeping in your bed and stuck in traffic. Traffic was the worst today. Nobody had cars and everyone was sleeping in bed, except those already at work who do not exist, because nobody exists.

After work, you decide that it is too early for breakfast. Since you are hungry, you decide to go for a jog. To brighten your day, you ask the annoying guy in the corner of the room if he would go running with you as you tie your shoes to your ears. It is a good thing you do not have ears, because that would look strange. Fortunately, everyone else wears their shoes on their ears, so you can keep wearing them on your feet. Much of your day is spent wishing you had shoes. But now that you have finished your breakfast, which is also lunch, it is time to leave for work. If only there was a way to get to work. Perhaps if you have breakfast again you would be at work.

This is only the beginning of the possibilities of the illogical state. In a static illogical state, the ink of a certain pen may be red and blue, but at least it would always be red and blue. If you found a route to work, you could always go that way. That route does not suddenly disappear in a static illogical state. In the illogical state, beings and objects relate to each other in one way, multiple ways, or not at all. Regardless of the logic state of God and people, they do relate to God. God has established a relationship with the physical universe, because in creating it, he interacted with it. Once an avenue for relationship between God and the physical is established, it remains.

If the world suddenly became illogical and transient, it would be immediately apparent. When testing the logic state of God, it would become immediately apparent if His state were illogical and transient. In a transient illogical state, all is almost lost. What is true today is not guaranteed for tomorrow. Truth is only applicable to any given

30

moment. Life would be a continuous relearning of everything people thought they knew. Fortunately, that is not the world we live in.

Regardless of God's state of logic, he has made it possible for people to relate with him. If God is logical, the depth of understanding and relating can be much deeper. To test whether God is logical or random, one must observe God's actions based on his projected character. If his actions correlate with a consistent character, then he is logical and acts based on his character. Every day science proves to a greater extent the predictability and logic of the physical universe. The logical, consistent constitution of all components of the physical universe indicates that God is most certainly logical. Until further experience proves otherwise, God can be understood to be logical, as there is a direct correlation between his character and his actions in creation. Humans can use logic to understand God through what they observe in the physical universe and through their own experiences.

Riddle: Can a God who can do anything create a rock that is too heavy for him to lift?

This is an interesting riddle that atheists enjoy challenging theists with. The point they are trying to prove is that it is impossible for a God who can do anything to exist. However, what they are admitting is that they cannot conceptualize the possibility of a God existing that resides outside of the logical state.

The ironic thing about this question is that it is possible for a logical God who can do anything to create a rock that is too heavy for him to lift. If God created a very small rock that had a very large mass, the rock would have a gravitational force great enough to suck the rest of the physical universe into it. If the entire physical universe were sucked into the rock, there would be no physical reference point other than the rock itself. If there is only one physical reference, all measurements must be taken from that reference. All measurements taken from the reference point of the rock to the position of the rock would show that the rock is always in the same position. If the rock is always in the same position, then it cannot move and thus cannot be lifted. So yes, a logical God who can do anything can create a rock that is too heavy for him to lift.

4   Why do we exist?

Meaning, Purpose, and Value

Those who gaze upon the magnificence of
God's creation and understand there is a being greater
than themselves, have taken their first step toward a
relationship with God. They take the second step when
—with curiosity and a genuine interest in who God is—
they begin an open search for him. Unfortunately,
many never search for God even though they believe he
exists. They are swept into the current of their familial
or cultural beliefs, or swept away in the struggles and
cares of life and make no time to search for God. But
God waits. The difficulties of life trouble and unsettle
people. When conflicts throw life out of balance,
people are unable to stabilize themselves. Faced with
uncertainty, insecurity, and instability, people begin to
ask probing questions and to reevaluate their beliefs.

They search for answers. They search for truth. This gives God opportunity to reveal himself to them.

People have taken many different paths in their search for God. One of those paths is the study of God's design of one's own being. By studying the design of something, the purpose for which it was created can be discovered. Design also indicates proper use and limitations. For example, when studying a bridge, one can deduce why it was built. The presence of a river, valley, or highway cutting between two points that the bridge connects identifies the purpose of the bridge. The presence of hand rails, guard rails, or railroad tracks indicate the particular use of the bridge. The size and strength of the bridge further outlines the intent for which it was designed. Studying the human constitution is similar.

When exhaust is produced by a car it has a reason for existence. The fuel composition, combustion, and after-treatment processes determine the existence and constitution of the exhaust. The cause of the exhaust, which is its reason for existence, is clear; but the exhaust has no purpose or value. The car, engine, and fuel all have purpose because they are designed to transport people from one place to another. The car, engine, and fuel have purpose and value. Their value is determined by the amount of money people are willing to pay for them. The exhaust has neither purpose nor value as it is a useless byproduct of the car. If the exhaust were useful or valuable it would be contained and used in some other process as opposed to being dissipated into the atmosphere. If an object is designed with intent, it has purpose. If someone interacts with an object in a positive significant manner, the object has value. The degree of value is determined by the people who sell or purchase the object.

The physical is determined by cause and effect. The actions and developments of physical systems are determined by their initial conditions. An object's reason for existence is rooted in its initial cause. Whether that cause was purposeful or accidental, every object has a reason for existence. However, having a reason for existence does not dictate purpose or value. An object is given purpose when designed and created to fulfill a particular need or desire. It is given value when some intelligent being estimates its ability to fulfill a need or desire. Because the physical is determined and has no will or desire of its own, a value generating being must have some nonphysical attribute or component.

Without a creator, the physical universe has no reason for being as it is. And without interaction with a nonphysical being, nothing in the universe has value. Whatever happens, happens. It does not matter what happens. It is all predetermined and will come to nothing in the end. The significance of the sun rising in the morning, a frog jumping off a lily pad, or a tree falling on two parents and orphaning their young children are all the same —absolutely zero. If the nonphysical does not exist and the universe is only physical, then humans would shrug and mumbled "that's life" in response to whatever news they receive.

Many people struggle with the idea of having no purpose, meaning, value, or significance. Humans have a fierce pride burning inside of them that rejects the notion that they are worthless. This pride reacts violently when someone belittles them. It drives people to achieve great things. It compels dictators and conquerors to strive for power and control. Pride insists that humans are more than physical objects and bares evidence accordingly. Physical objects do not care who is the most famous, most powerful, or most influential, but prideful beings do. A piece of granite does not care that it is not gold. The grass does not care that the trees stand taller. The Indian Ocean does not care about the size of the Pacific Ocean. But humans care. Humans are driven by a desire for significance and value. They are more than physical bodies. They have a nonphysical component that drives them to search for purpose and meaning.

The ever continuous search for knowledge further substantiates that humans are more than cause and effect of a predetermined physical world. Humans search for knowledge because they believe it is valuable. If they obtain some knowledge not yet discovered or disseminate knowledge to those who lack it, then they have accomplished a valuable task. Those searching for knowledge believe that increased knowledge leads to improved lives. However, such a statement requires a comparison of value between one life and another. It assumes that life and comfort and pleasure have some value. There is no difference in value between a rock basking in the sun or frozen in the arctic, soothed in a cool stream or riding a lava flow. Any estimation of value describing one experience of life as better or more desirable than another requires an estimation of value. For humans to evaluate what conditions of life are best and search for knowledge to improve their conditions, they must be more than just the physical. They must have a nonphysical component.

Humans have at least two components: the physical body and the nonphysical soul. Souls consider and imagine, and the body is the tool by which a soul gathers information concerning the physical universe. The body has five types of sensors which gather information and relay it back to the soul: sight, sound, smell, touch, and taste. These senses are useful for the protection and enjoyment of physical life, but they also allow for interaction between souls and for development of relationships. Without the physical, relationships are

37

static. They do not form; they do not break; they do not grow or develop. The physical allows humans to form relationships with each other and with God.

As useful as the body is, it is just an object. Objects are created and function according to their design with no input of their own. It is not responsible for anything it does because it is designed for a purpose and controlled by external forces. It acts according to its construct and the governing laws of science. It has no capacity to change its constitution. An object has no rights or responsibilities. It is property. Responsibility for what an object is and does lies with its architect, builder, director, and motivator. As God is the creator of the entire physical universe, he is the ultimate creator of the physical body. He is responsible for what the body is, but he has given the physical body to the human soul to inhabit and possess. The human soul controls and operates the physical body it possesses. Thus, it is the human soul which has responsibility for what the body does and becomes. Humans are responsible to God for that which they do in their bodies.

Since God created the body and gave it to the soul, one might ask "Where did self come from?" "How did I become me?" "Did God created me to be me?" "Is God ultimately responsible for everything I do?"

The soul has the attribute of independent constitution. That means it defines itself and nothing determines what it must be or become. Because it is nonphysical, it is not dependent on anything else, but can choose what it will become. Whether God created the human soul or not does not change this. A fish, when released into the water, chooses where it goes next. A soul, when set free, chooses what it becomes next. The human self, while it may have come into existence by the will of God, determines its own future. The soul is responsible for what it becomes.

The soul is limited to what it will become only by the limits of its knowledge and imagination. Fortunately for humans, they also have bodies. Through physical senses, the body experiences new possibilities, learns about others, and develops relationship with others. All of these give the soul the opportunity to become something different of its own choosing.

Some will reject the concept of humans having independent constitution and insist that God is responsible for everything they do and insist it is God's fault that they are who they are. If such is the case, they should submit themselves to God's will to do everything he commands, directs, and desires. They should be made into whatever God desires. When submitted to God, God is responsible. However, if an individual will not submit to God and protest, "I enjoy what I do" or "I like who I am" or "I want what I have," then he is expressing a desire to maintain his own will and responsibility for his life. He claims he can live better without God's direction, or become greater than the transformation God would accomplish in him, or obtain more than what God would give. Those expressions of the soul are nothing more than expressions of pride. Such an expression shows both its independent constitution and inconsistence with God's character.

Creating Value

If a soul can fulfill some unique or significant role. Then it has value and meaning. This available path to value and significance drives many to strive for uniqueness. The drive for value through uniqueness is all that is needed to send human minds into creativity. As they imagine, dream, create, and invent, they produce that which could only come from them. Without them, the world would not be the same. The evidence of value creation through uniqueness is seen in the rewards lavished upon those who excel through skill, intelligence, and creativity in every segment of life, including government, academia, athletics, entertainment, art, and business. Doing something no one else can do or has done produces value for self.

The development of uniqueness is accomplished through creating or relating. If someone dedicates himself to creating some object or accomplishing some task that is esteemed valuable by others, then that person obtains significance and purpose. That person has taken his existence and committed it to the fulfillment of some task not already fulfilled by someone else. They have chosen to serve. It is not the idea of doing some menial task. It is the idea of an Einstein or Mozart or Martin Luther King Jr., who, if he fails to fulfill his role, would be missed, whose shoes would remain empty. By relating with others, people impact others and fulfill needs. The greater their impact and more unique their fulfillment, the more purpose and value they obtain for themselves. Unlike people, objects cannot create purpose for themselves. It can only be given to them by a being with a nonphysical component.

It is not a lack or deficiency in the character of a person that causes him to search for purpose and value; it is the nature of his character. If someone no longer creates or relates, he would become a spot with no connection to anything. Perhaps the nonphysical world is filled with spots, but nobody knows they exist and nobody cares, not even the spots themselves. They are happy being spots, forever transfixed in isolation. Some humans try to become spots through meditation, emptying their minds of everything, and the suppression of all desires, even the desires to fulfill the physical needs of the body. Perhaps some have even reached their desired point of nothingness where they void themselves of all desire, purpose, value, and relationship before they physically die and lose even the comforts and relationships a physical body affords; at which point they are forever isolated, whether they like it or not.

Others, instead of attempting to create purpose for themselves, turn to amusement. They avoid pondering their purpose; focusing instead on pleasure. But they cannot achieve lasting contentment through such pursuits. It would require an ever increasing volume of distractions, novelties, pleasures, and entertainment. When they run out of distractions and find nothing else to captivate their attention, they will become bored and begin to think. Then it is not long until they realize they need a reason for existence, a purpose of existence, or some value in existence. Upon such a realization, they start searching for answers and fulfillment.

God's Motivations for Creating the Physical

Had God desired to be a spot and find contentment in the amusement of his own thoughts and imagination, the physical universe would never have existed. God never would have been motivated to create. Instead, God was motivated to design and create an intricate life-supporting universe with people to whom he could relate. To understand God, it is essential to know why he created such a world or what motivated him to create it.

There are two great motivators that could cause a supreme being to create: pride and love. Pride and love are opposites. Pride is the positive estimation of self. Love is the positive estimation of others. Pride tries to raise up self while putting down others. Love seeks to promote others while humbling self. Pride wants to be served; love wants to serve. Pride promotes self; love sacrifices for others.

To determine God's motive in creating the world, one must study the result of God's actions. The results of pride and love are always opposite. Pride destroys. It tears down communities. It disrupts relationships. It constantly pushes a wedge between people because pride always tries to elevate self. It drives the one up and the other down. With such division, relationships are destroyed. When two people love each other, they try to build each other up. Not in a competitive way, but in a harmonious, unified way. It results in them humbly serving each other and working together. That unity and togetherness strengthens their relationship and produces wonderful results. If actions destroy relationships, then they are motivated by pride.

If they create and strengthen relationships, then they are motivated by love.

Consider again the human constitution. It has a soul which allows it the capacity for relationships. As opposed to objects which cannot have relationships because they are not responsible for their actions. Humans, because of their souls, are responsible for their actions and thus may choose to enter into relationships. This is essential for relationships. The human constitution also has a body which allows for the ability to form relationships. Through the body, humans learn and interact with other beings. This is necessary for relationships.

A third component of the humans constitution is the conscience which is key for creating relationships. Conscience gives people the ability to recognize a conflict between what one wants to do and what one ought to do. It allows people to recognize the difference between their desires and values and the desires and values of others, and particularly of God. In a relationship, two people put themselves in a situation where they must depend on each other. They depend on each other to understand what is important and necessary, to protect the relationship and each other. If a person lacks a conscience, he is unable to evaluate whether or not his desires align with the needs, values, desires, and expectations of the other person. If two people enter a relationship and one of them lacks a conscience, then that relationship becomes nothing more than the person with a conscience assisting the other person in fulfilling his own desires. If neither person has a conscience, then the relationship disintegrates into each using the other to satisfy their own desires. The conscience helps the soul transform into what it must become in order to have a relationship with God.

If God was motivated by pride to create the universe, then the universe would be designed in such a way that all creation would be driven into submission while God is elevated. But if God was motivated by love, then the universe will be such that God may establish relationships with other beings. The first indications of God being motivated by love are in the human constitution. Further indications will be discussed in the following two chapters.

5 Why do people suffer and die?

The world is a mess. With sickness, suffering, famine, injustice, corruption, etc. there seems to be no end of misery. Everywhere these are unhappy people, people searching for love, hope, purpose, comfort, peace, success, and joy. And so few seem to find it. Why would God allow all of this to happen?

If humans designed a world, it would be perfect: no suffering, no death, pure joy and happiness. It would be an eternal paradise. All physical needs would be supplied, work would be unnecessary and people would have unlimited time to do whatever they want. There would be no strife or conflict. There would be no sorrow or struggles. There would be no pain or death. That is a world that makes sense. But that is not the world that exists today. What went wrong? Why does God's apparent plan for the universe appear so different from what human's would plan? The answers to these questions begin with a look into the formation of ethics.

Formation of Ethics

Ethics arise from the interactions of beings who posses both desires and conscience. Each individual has a set of values by which he appreciates or depreciates everything in his life. As people interact and establish community, the things they collectively value become the most important to the community. Those things of greatest importance are those which need protection most. As societies and individuals organically work through the process of determining degrees of value and alignment of needs and desires, a set of standard behaviors emerge, so that which is valuable may be protected. The set of valuables that need protection is the beginning of a code of ethics. Actions that protect and promote that which is valuable are considered ethical; actions that endanger them are considered unethical.

There is not always agreement upon what is most valuable. Pride causes people to place value on themselves; desire or lust causes them to place value on external objects as their personality dictates. When individuals come together, there are differences. These differences are compounded by differences in goals, responsibilities, education, background, and perspective. When differences cannot be settled, those with the most authority, power, or support set precedence.

Throughout societies, communities, families, and individuals, layers of ethical codes develop. A society may establish a set of ethical standards and within that, a community may establish additional standards. Within the community, a family may refine the standards. Finally, at the individual level, people may establish their ultimate personal code of ethics.

For example, a society decides that human life is important and must be protected. Therefore, they declare murder a violation of the society's code of ethics. However, assault, abuse, and fighting are permitted. That society has decided that the strong may triumph over the weak and exploit them as long as no one is killed. Within that society, there is a community which recognizes that people are more industrial and that the economy grows when people and property are protected. They believe life is better if the weak are protected and no one is exploited. In addition to the societal prohibition of murder, that community adds a prohibition against assault and abuse within their community. Within that community, fighting to defending one's honor is acceptable. Organized duels and gang brawls are permitted, provided no one is murdered or abused. But within that community, a family decides that forgiveness and peace are more valuable than honor and revenge. They decide that they will not fight and will teach their children to be peaceful. For that family, not only murder and abuse are prohibited, but fighting is also forbidden. Within that family, an individual may add even another layer to his code of ethics. Recognizing that fighting is often preceded by anger, because anger clouds judgment and causes lack of self control, that individual decides that anger is unacceptable and so forbids himself from ever expressing angry. In this society, four layers of codes compose the code of ethics which govern the behavior of an individual.

This establishment of ethics works until an individual or subgroup of society rejects some standard of behavior. If this happens, the affected society or community may choose either to modify what they consider ethical or enforce their standards by establishing a system of laws and consequences to protect what they consider valuable. By establishing laws, they declare what they consider valuable, how those valuables ought to be treated, and the consequences for mistreating the valuables.

God, as a being with values, also desires to protect what he values through a system of laws and consequences. To understand the ethical standards of God, one should determine what God values and the manner in which those values can be protected. Beings place value on themselves, on things with which they interact meaningfully, and things which they use to achieve their goals. That means God values four particular things: himself, humans beings (with whom God desires to have a relationship), the physical universe (which facilitates a relationship between God and people), and physical human life (which affords God opportunity to establish a relationship). God's system of laws and the design of the universe are for the promotion of that which God values.

The Problems with Paradise

The desire for a utopian world that fulfills human desires and meets all human needs is motivated by the desire to please self. When people are unhappy with what they have or what they experience, they desire a better, utopian world where all humans needs and desires are satisfied. Unfortunately, in such a world, when the focus of one's life is self-gratification, there is no room for relationship. Even if relationships are desired, there is no opportunity for them to grow. Relationships need trust and sacrifice; but if everything is easy and abundant, there is little or no opportunity for the expression of trust or sacrifice. Relationship form when there is need or want. They thrive in times of conflict or danger, when people recognize their weaknesses and their need for relationships. People need to depend on each other and trust each other for relationships form. Trusting another person leaves an individual vulnerable to the other. Unless there is need, conflict, or danger, people do not trust each other. As a relationship forms, external conflict brings the individuals together. As conflicts arise and multiply, the individuals develop a greater understanding of their need for each other, a greater appreciation for each other's character, and a greater willingness to trust and to sacrifice for each other. This understanding of one's own weaknesses and of another's strengths translates into humility and love. It is humility and love which form relationships, not a paradise world of self-gratification.

The opposites of humility and love are pride and lust, which destroy relationships. Humility is manifested either in admitting the need for assistance or in willingness to take a low place and serve another. Love is manifested in the sacrifice of one's own desire and will for the benefit or support of another. When humility and love are exercised, a relationship grows; but when pride or lust invades, a relationship crumbles. Pride promotes self at the cost of serving others. Lust desires to please self at the cost of sacrificing for others. Both pride and lust are self-focused and devalue others.

In a paradise where lust and pride may flourish without consequence, relationships are meaningless. They become nothing more that the momentary interaction between two individuals for the purpose of gratifying their own lusts. Nothing binds them together; the desire to please self presses them together for a moment before they separate. When either person becomes unsatisfied or bored with what he is receiving, he leaves and finds someone else. There is no trust, no faithfulness, and no commitment. There is no relationship. As frivolous and short as the momentary interactions between two humans would become, there would be even less interaction between people and God. In a paradise where all needs and desires are met, there is no need for God. God creates paradise – end of story. He is no longer needed.

Perhaps if the human-designed paradise was relaxed a bit to allow a few conflicts, surely then relationships could form and all would be perfect. There would still be no death or major catastrophes, but there would be limited resources to create some conflict. People would need to learn to depend on each other, do at least some minimal work, and cooperate with each other. The world would be great, until the rise of cliques and clans. They would vie with each other over the limited resources until a dominant group gained control. Everyone opposed to the group in power would be subjugated and submitted to the demands of the dominant group. Within the dominant group, conflict would arise between the leading heads. After a power struggle, the most powerful, intelligent, and influential would conquer his adversaries and establish himself as a dictator. The whole world would be put into servitude and would exist for the fulfillment of the desires and whims of the supreme dictator. In time, perhaps others would rise up, but the rest of the world would remain in eternal servitude, not even set free by way of death. Life itself would drudge by until the needs of the earth's population exceed the available resources. They would all live an eternity of starvation and slavery devoid of joy or purpose. What happened to paradise? A world where people are permitted to do whatever they want will result in ruin and misery for the masses without even the hope of escaping by death. God would be distant, helpless, and unworthy of trust.

Perhaps if everyone were nice and did what they should, a wonderful world of relationships would exist, like a virus-free network of computers. All selfish desires would be suppressed; people would be programmed to do what is right. That would be paradise. But if such were the case, the universe would be no more than physical objects, devoid of self-desire or self-will. Everyone would function as designed, and the whole system would function harmoniously. There would be a peaceful world, but relationships would not exist. Relationships cannot exist without the existence of self-desire and self-will. People need personality and the ability to decide if they want a relationship; if so, with whom to have a relationship. This ability to choose comes with the ability to choose self in pride or lust over all others.

Humans desire a world without pain, suffering, and death. However, for God to create a world with the purpose of establishing love relationships, he must avoid the three scenarios just presented: a paradise where lust and pride may flourish without consequence, a free society where a selfish individual can subjugate the masses to eternal slavery, and a programmed lifeless universe devoid of free will and choice. In each of those cases, establishing relationships between God and people becomes impossible.

Designed for Relationships

God must allow for some limitations of paradise or the entrance of some imperfection into paradise to achieve his ultimate goals. When paradise fails to satisfy the lusts of an individual, he ponders his own existence and desires purpose and value. He sees that life is more than self and that relationships with others would be meaningful. Or when paradise is disrupted and suffering is permitted to enter and people find themselves in danger they cannot avoid, they turn to others for help. As soon as pleasure is denied and suffering or danger enters, relationships make sense. People become bound together in relationships as soon as physical needs and desire for purpose bring them together. Need, uncertainty, and danger often also cause people to search for their creator and desire a relationship with him. This is particularly true when society is unable or unwilling to meet the needs of an individual or fails to give an individual purpose in life.

God must prevent the eternal reign of a dictator. An eternal dictator is permitted to dominate in a free society when there is no active authority above human government. In a free society, God permits people to do whatever they want without interference, so when someone conquers the world, God does not intervene or liberate the world. To maintain some degree of order and balance in the world, God must introduce another component into the system that keeps it in equilibrium. With some addition, God must ensure that people are ultimately responsible to him and yet have the liberty to choose whether or not they want a relationship with him. If every action contrary to the character and desire of God and his design for the universe were corrected or punished immediately, everyone would be forced into submission or banished from God's universe. If such were the case, a consensual loving relationship with God would be impossible.

To maintain a world where people are ultimately held responsible to God and yet still have liberty and expression of self, God must introduce death into the world as the consequence or punishment for actions contrary to God's ethical standard. This would prevent an eternal dictator. Despite the greater position, power, or prestige one individual may achieve over another, in death, all are made equal and all are responsible to God. While people have life, they can act as they please. In life, they may accept or deny God's invitation for a relationship, but God has decreed that there will be a time when each person must give account to God.

In God's value system, a relationship with individuals is more important than physical life. God does value physical life, for he designed and created it, and gains through it relationships with people. However, if physical life were protected to such an extent that relationships become impossible and life itself becomes slavery, life loses all value. If someone buys a shovel to dig a hole, but never uses that shovel for fear of breaking it, the shovel has no value. The value of physical life is in its potential for relationship, so if a life cannot achieve its goal, it is useless.

God must as well not create a programmed lifeless universe. If God had wanted a lovely movie, he could have programmed everyone to do exactly what they should do. No one hurts anyone, everyone falls in love and everything ends happily ever after. Unfortunately, in such a world there would be no true relationships. They would only be for show. Or if God designed a world which ran like a computer program with everything working harmoniously, there would still be no true relationships. Relationships would be lifeless. For a relationship to exist, people must be allowed to act based on their own desires without being coerced. Unfortunately, that means people may behave contrary to the values and desire of others. That means people can endanger and destroy that which is considered valuable by others. That means people living in God's world may abuse those things God values.

The Present Reality

The present reality is certainly not the paradise humans would have designed. However, God has designed and created a world where human deviance from God's plan and desires is permitted, and through which he can obtain relationships with people. As a consequence, conflict, suffering, and death are permitted when lust and pride are expressed. In such a world, the innocent suffer and infants die –not because God likes suffering and death, but because he understands that something greater than the comforts of physical life can be gained. God desires beautiful, enjoyable, harmonious relationships with people and between people; but the lust and pride of individuals ruin all that is beautiful causing suffering, sorrow, and death.

A world of deviance, conflict, suffering, and death is the world that exists. This world was not designed to encourage terrible things, but does allow for them because of what may be gained. If God had wanted a world with a hamster that eats, sleeps, and runs on its wheel for eternity, he could have created a comfortable world for it; however, that is not what he created. But, because God wants relationships and this physical life is only temporary, there is hope. There must be something after physical death. God does not establish relationships with people on earth to have them die, and terminate the relationship. If death ends relationships, then God is left with nothing when the physical universe runs into equilibrium. The physical universe is temporary, but God has plans to gain from it that which is eternal. Physical death is the end of opportunity, but not the end of existence. When someone dies, he loses everything physical; but if he has developed a relationship with God while alive, he continues his relationship with God after death.

A life of joy, satisfaction, and fulfillment is never obtained by feeding lust and pride. Lust and pride are only ever satisfied for a moment, but humans continue on. Striving for a fulfilled life through momentary pleasures creates a life of endless thirst for more. A life of joy, satisfaction, and fulfillment is not obtained with a life of comfort, safety, and ease. When physical needs are met, the human soul cries louder longing for meaning, purpose, and value. It requires a relationship with God to complete life. A relationship with God establishes something of eternal value for both the individual and for God. It gives eternal meaning, purpose, and value to self. The human soul finds joy, satisfaction, and fulfillment in a relationship with God.

Some will still object that God is unjust in allowing the innocent to suffer. This only shows the difference in values between God and the objectors. That which is right and just, must adhere to a code of ethics. Ethical codes are established by what is considered valuable. A physical life of comfort without suffering is not what is most valuable in God's eyes. He values relationships, which are strengthened through suffering. God is just when he permits suffering, because it allows for the formation of what God values most. Those who are unsatisfied with life or angered by God because He allows the world to exist as it does today are those who lack a relationship with God because of their pride and lust. God offers everyone joy, satisfaction, and fulfillment, but one must let go of self and turn to God in humility, trust and love. Humans tend to focus just on this physical life. God is looking beyond this life and thus his value system encompasses more than the physical we experience today.

6 Can we escape judgment and punishment?

The Function of Law

As architect, builder, and proprietor of the physical universe, it is God's prerogative to set the ethical standard for everything within his universe. When he gave physical bodies to human souls and placed them in the physical universe, they became responsible to him for everything that they do in it. As independent souls, humans may choose to conform to God's ethical standard or ignore it. However, if they reject God's standard, behaving as dictated by their own character, they jeopardize what God values. To protect what he values, God has the authority to establish laws and enforce them.

A law has the power to protect that which is valuable by discouraging people from committing an offense and by preventing people from repeating an offense. The law discourages people from breaking the law by threatening to punish offenders. If an individual is not dissuaded but commits an offense, then the law has two responsibilities. If it fulfills both these responsibilities, then it remains an effective law. The first is to carry out the prescribed punishment. This neither rights the wrong which was done nor establishes justice, but it teaches others the consequence of an offense with the goal that others will beware and refrain from committing the same offense. It is important to understand that the law does not justify. Rarely does the price exacted from the offender fully compensate for the trespass or crime committed; nor does the law have the power to force an offender to repent and become aligned in their character with the ethical standard. Law may prevent an offense, but it cannot undo an offense.

The second responsibility of the law is to prevent an offender from repeating an offense. The most complete fulfillment of this responsibility is to accomplish repentance in the offender, but the law has difficulty doing so. In repentance, the offender changes his mind to agree with the purpose of the law. The offender's desires are changed to value what the law protects. If repentance occurs, the law is no longer necessary; for that individual is now committed to protect that which he once endangered. The law may encourage repentance through education, but it cannot ensure an individual has repented. Because the law cannot ensure repentance, it has the responsibility of preventing an unrepentant offender from repeating the offense. This is done through restraint such as prison or incapacitation such as execution. Repeated offenses underscore the ineffectiveness of a law and its consequences.

God values himself, humans, and his relationships with humans, so the laws he establishes are laws which will protect these things. Lust and pride are the greatest threats to what God values. God uses suffering and death as consequences for wrongful actions motivated by lust and pride. Suffering and death are not necessarily part of God's creatorial design, but are the result of actions contrary to the values and standards of God. Suffering warns that death may result from the present behavior and is a tool of a merciful God who desires repentance. Death is a persuasive tool for discouraging trespass and an enforcing tool for preventing a repeated offense.

When an individual acts contrary to a law, he is bound under the law to be punished with the consequences of that law. Should an individual be set free from the law without both responsibilities of the law fulfilled, the law becomes powerless and void. When someone breaks one of God's laws, he becomes bound under God's law. Anytime an individual acts out of lust or pride, he endangers what God values and breaks God's law. It is the natural desire of humans to act out of lust and pride against the desires of God, so by nature, every human becomes bound under the law of God. The evidence of this is seen in the course of human life. Everyone dies; no one lives forever. If someone could live perfectly, perhaps they could live forever. But amongst all the multitudes of earth, no one has ever escaped death.

There are two causes of death in regard to the law: it results either from the unjust action of an individual exerting his self-will or it is the punishment for one's own crime. Therefore, it is possible for an innocent person to die. He dies as a result of the crime of another. Each must evaluate the condition of his own heart as to whether it contains lust or pride. If lust or pride is discovered as the motivation of any action, he is guilty and bound under the law of God. The law and the conscience work together and reveal to individuals the waywardness of their character. People desire wonderful lives without suffering and death, but this is unachievable because people, by nature, ignore God's law and fall under its consequences.

Death is the ultimate consequence for breaking God's law. It is tragic when someone dies, especially if they have not repented and have no relationship with God. When they die, they lose the opportunity to establish a relationship with God. Physical death is the final stroke of the law. If the law loses its power or effectiveness, then the whole law is useless. Because of the seriousness of death and eternal separation, the law points people to God, while they are still alive, as their opportunity to escape. The law is unable to save people from consequences, but it warns them that judgment is coming and gives opportunity to flee to God.

The Need for Repentance

Humans naturally act against the values, desires, and character of God. Thus, four things must take place for God and an individual to establish a relationship: repentance, redemption, forgiveness, and justification.

Repentance is required because a person's natural state of mind conflicts with God. Two individuals with opposing values, desires, or goals cannot have a love relationship.

Redemption is required because every human is under condemnation of the law for their trespasses, and thus has forfeited their right to life. So for God to gain an eternal relationship, he must pay the penalty for trespasses against the law to set that life free from the law.

Forgiveness is required because in trespassing the law, every human has offended God; they have acted unfaithfully.

Justification is required because God needs to be able to trust an individual to protect that which is valuable. Without that trust, a relationship is impossible.

Repentance is not an act that is done and forgotten, but a transformation experienced in the core of an individual. It is accomplished, not through the lusts of the heart, but by the humbling of the mind. Repentance is not a remorseful apology for getting caught. It is a complete change of attitude and values. In the natural human state, people care most about themselves as expressed through pride and lust, which destroy every relationship. Repentance from that state gives priority to God and a relationship with him, which is expressed through love and humility. God already loves people and desires a relationship, so humans must adopt God's position for a relationship between them to develop.

Satisfying the Law through Substitution

When an individual repents, he could begin a relationship with God, except that the law has placed a barrier between him and God. Regardless of the desires of God, he established a law that cannot be broken. Retracting or changing the law would require changing God's character, making him a liar, inhibiting future relationships, and voiding present relationships. Sidestepping the law is not possible. The law must be carried out to facilitate the achievement of God's goal for relationships. To give a repentant individual eternal life by evading death or through resurrection from the dead, God must redeem him from the condemnation of the law. For God to redeem individuals from the responsibilities of the law and the consequence of breaking the law, the penalty of death must be exacted, as the law demands. This is accomplished by the substitution of a physical life for the lives of others.

Substitution does not skirt the law. The law must fulfill two responsibilities when a trespass occurs: first, ensure that the offender does not repeat the offense; second, teach others the gravity of committing the same trespass. If repentance occurs, the first responsibility is satisfied. When severity of the consequence is demonstrated, the second responsibility is satisfied. The law accomplishes this through the punishment of the offender or the punishment of a willing and able substitute. An example of this is the payment of a fine. When an offender is given a fine, there is no requirement about who pays the fine. It could be the offender or any other willing and able individual. Regardless of who pays the fine, the full cost and consequence of the trespass has been exacted. Thus the law maintains its power.

The concept of substitution may unsettle some for two reasons. The first reason is the desire to inflict pain as punishment and revenge. This is due to the pride of self-centered people. Pride says, "If I am offended, humiliated, or hurt, then I want the offender to be offended, humiliated, and hurt. I want him to suffer." This is not justice; it is revenge. Justice rights a wrong or restores a loss. Revenge purposefully destroys someone or something without righting the wrong or restoring the loss. Revenge does not promote that which is valued.

The second reason substitution may be unsettling comes from a misunderstanding of repentance. For the law to be satisfied, repentance must always accompany substitution. Punishment should dissuade an individual from repeating the offense and dissuade others from following in the path of the offender. If the offender repents, then punishment does not decrease the chances of a repeat offense because the repentant individual no longer has the desire or motivation to repeat the offense. Once repentance occurs, punishment only serves to dissuade others, which can be accomplished through the punishment of a qualified substitute.

God as the Substitute

Repentance is the responsibility of the offender. God may encourage an individual's repentance, but it is the individual who decides if he will repent. If an individual repents, then it is God's responsibility to redeem that individual from the sentence of death. When a human breaks the law, he forfeits his life. Since he has no power in himself to regain his life, he cannot save himself. Nor can another human redeem him, for everyone has forfeited his own life through trespass of the law. God, being perfect, is the only being not under condemnation of the law and whose life is not forfeited. God himself must become the substitute to establish a relationship with people.

Someone might suggest that an animal would qualify as an acceptable substitute. While animals may not be under the condemnation of the law, they are unable to be willing substitutes. A substitute must understand both the offense and the consequences. They must understand both the punishment and the reason for it. Limited communication between humans and animals disqualifies them as acceptable substitutes.

The sentence of death does not result in nonexistence. The sentence is that of physical death. For God to die physically as a substitute for humans, he must first have become physical; he must have inhabited a physical form. The idea of God entering into his own creation angers some because they believe it diminishes God; however, an idea only diminishes God if it conflicts with God's character. God becoming physical so that he might be a substitute for humans does not diminish God if such an action is consistent with his character. Becoming physical for substitution is consistent with the character of a God who desires a relationship with people; it is required for God to gain a relationship with people. One must understand that if God becomes human, he does not become any less God. Humans are a combination of soul and physical body. The physical body does not diminish the character of the soul in any way. God is a soul with power and authority over the entire physical universe. God does not lose his character, power, or authority by taking on a physical body. The only changes that occurs by God taking on a physical body is that God is able to die physically if he so chooses. The souls of God and of humans do not depend on the life of the physical body. When the human body dies, the soul continues to live.

70

So if God physically dies after assuming a physical body, he continues as God. Furthermore, if God dies physically as a substitute, he still has the power and authority to take a physical form again. Such power and authority is not dependent on his physical state, but on his nonphysical character, which remains unaffected by that which occurs in a physical body.

One might postulate that for God to substitute himself for every repentant individual, he must repeat death for each one. However, neither substitution nor the law requires this. Substitution is only the idea of something taking the place of something else. In sports, when one player subs-in for another player, it is not necessary that they be equal in ability. In calculus, when doing U-substitution, there is nothing wrong with substituting u for $4x^3+5x^2+9$. If three people are held hostage, an agreement may be reached to substitute one person for all three. In substitution, the only necessity is that all invested parties are satisfied with the substitution. Provided that all invested parties are in agreement, any substitution may be transacted, regardless of value, quantity, or character. In the substitution of God for a human individual, three parties must be satisfied: God, the individual, and the law.

As already noted, the law has two requirements when an offense occurs: the dissuasion of the individual from repeating the offense and the demonstration to others of the consequence of the offense. When a willing substitute receives punishment for a repentant offender, the law is satisfied. Therefore, if God willingly dies physically once, he is able to be the substitute for every repentant individual who accepts his substitution.

A common objection to this concept of repentance and substitution is that an individual can do whatever he wants and still escape punishment, as long as he repents. This objection stems from a wrong understanding of either repentance or of the purpose of the law. If an individual has truly repented from an action, he will not repeat it. Repentance is a change in values achieved through education. When an individual repents, he has a new understanding of what is valuable. This change in values will always result in a change of desires, motivations, intentions, and actions. If an individual commits an offense and claims repentance but repeats the offense, then it is obvious that repentance had never occurred. Likely what occurred was remorse, regret, or shame; these are rooted in emotion produced by unintended or undesired consequence. When someone is caught and punished, they may regret committing the crime, not because they see it as wrong, but because they suffered punishment for it. Or someone may regret committing a crime if they accidentally hurt someone they love in the commission of the crime. In either example, there is no change in motivation for committing the original offense. The goal of the law is to keep someone from committing an offense or repeating it; so if repentance occurs, the offense will not be repeated by the individual and the law has accomplished its goal in regard to that individual.

There is also the objection that someone could commit a lifetime of offenses with the intent of repenting at the end knowing that by substitution he will go unpunished. The fallacy of this hypothetical situation lies in the impossibility of intending to repent without immediately repenting. Intention is a mindset and repentance is a change of mindset. Someone's mindset changes when he decides to take a different course. If someone intends to repent, he is of the mindset of changing his mindset. When someone decides he will change his mind, he has, at that moment, already changed his mind. The idea of deciding to repent is a redundant thought because that decision requires repentance itself. If someone says he plans to repent in the future, he is lying; for he claims he intends to intend the opposite of what he currently intends. In reality, what he means is: once he fulfills his present desire, he believes he will be satisfied and then will do whatever he should have done in the first place. That is not repentance.

There is another difficulty with the idea of intending to repent with the hope of evading punishment. No one knows when judgment will come. No individual has control over the length of his life. While he may make wise decisions to prevent a certain early demise, there are still many occasions for death that he cannot control. Regardless of one's intentions, the substitution of God is irrelevant until true repentance has occurred.

The substitution of God for individuals does more than redeem them from the condemnation of the law and give them the ability to have life and a relationship with God. God's act of substitution demonstrates love through personal sacrifice for the individual. In dying as a substitute for humans, God goes beyond the demands of the law, but in doing so he fulfills the law, for he removes every barrier of a relationship between God and humans.

Forgiveness and Faith

When an individual repents, his values align with God's values; the substitution of God redeems him from the consequences of the law. However, for a relationship to exist, forgiveness must occur. In the process of breaking the law through actions motivated by lust and pride, humans have offended God. Even though the law is satisfied, it takes a separate conscious decision of God to forgive. The forgiveness of God is undeserved and would be unexpected, except for God's character of love and his desire for a relationship. Pride prevents relationships and stands in the way of forgiveness. One who humbles himself to die as a substitute can be depended upon to forgive.

Relationship requires a harmony of character and value and the demonstration of love. It also requires faith and faithfulness. Faith depends on the promise and character of another. Faithfulness is the fulfillment of one's promise and projected character. At two points in the establishing of a relationship between God and an individual, the individual must have faith in the character of God: in trusting that God will act as his substitute in death and in trusting that God will forgive. While the events of substitution and forgiveness may be supported by historical evidence, the reality of them depends on the character of God. If God is as he projects himself to be through the physical world, then he will be the substitute and he will forgive. Therefore, a relationship is established when a repentant individual trusts in the character of God.

The transience of God is important to faithfulness. God's character at the creation of the universe can be understood through the present conditions of the universe. But what if God has changed? Or what if God no longer cares? Or what if we made a mistake and misunderstood who God is? The answer to all these questions is the same. Once a hypothesis for the character of God is reached, it needs to be tested. Call out to God on the basis of the hypothesis in faith and repentance and see if God responds. If there is no response, then begin reevaluating who God is. But if the hypothesis is correct, God will respond. This communication with God and evidence of his character will be further discussed in the next chapter.

The Finale of Justification

The marvelous outcome of having faith in God is justification. Justification restores that which has been wrongfully taken away and corrects the values of the offending party. By having faith in God, an individual accomplishes what the law tried to protect: a relationship with God. Faith is the essence of relationship. It is the willing dependence of one person on another and confidence in the love, character, and abilities of the other. Those who have faith in God have come to know him and have confidence in him.

With repentance, substitution, faith, and justification accomplished, there is nothing left to prevent a relationship between God and an individual.

The law and conscience have shown the error and consequence of human pride and lust. Human repentance has aligned the individual with God. God's willing substitution gives him the right to redeem repentant individuals from the consequences of the law. Through his death, God has demonstrated his love and willingness to forgive. Faith in the character of God justifies the individual as God and the individual become one in values, desires, and character. This unity is the beginning of an eternal relationship which shall extend beyond the existence of a temporary, physical world. With characters aligned with God, humans are able to enjoy God's presence and blessings for an eternity of relating and creating.

But what would God do to someone who still denies and rejects him? There is nothing more God could do to establish a relationship. God has demonstrated love, grace, and mercy through sacrifice, humility, and patience. There is only one thing God could do –remove himself from the presence of such an individual. When God's presence leaves, all that God created goes with it. When God removes himself from someone who has rejected him, that soul enters an abyss devoid of all comfort, joy, love, friendship, and company. He is forever alone, forever tormented by his crimes and their consequences and by the possibilities of what could have been. But for those who repent and trust, there is joy, love, and life in the presence of God forever.

7   How do we find God?

The Need for Communication

While God has provided all the necessities for establishing a relationship when he designed and created the physical universe (including human beings with body, conscience, and intellect), there is one relational component creation does not supply: communication. Communication transfers information from one party to another without repeating the experience through which the information was gained.

Individuals must communicate to obtain information they have not gathered or cannot gather through experience. This is particularly true for forming relationships. The knowledge of an individual's character, desires, and values can be transferred from one person to another through communication or through physical interaction. When physical interaction occurs without communication and outside of an established relationship, it is invasion of personal space and possibly assault. This could be a sudden kiss from a stranger or a push on a crowded bus. Rarely is physical interaction without communication desirable. Relationships must begin with communication. For God to establish a relationship with people, they need knowledge of his character, desires, and values. They obtain these through communication. Some argue, "If God wants me to know him, why doesn't he reveal himself in some unambiguous way? " For God to reveal himself and make his character and desires unambiguous for an individual with whom he lacks a relationship, he would have to forcibly impress upon that individual all the attributes and values of God. His full power and majesty would be impressed upon them. God's moral standard would overwhelm them when faced with their failure to comply with it. This would result either in eternal expulsion of the individual from God's presence or immediate submission and servitude of the individual to God; it would be an assault by God on the individual. If God made himself suddenly known to an individual with whom he had no previous relationship, it would result in the loss of any opportunity to establish a relationship with that individual. Relationships require knowledge, faith, and consensual alignment of values. This can only be obtained through communication.

Knowledge obtained through science is knowledge obtained by experience. Scientific assertions stand or fall based on verification by experience or experiment. If an assertion conflicts with experience, then the assertion is regarded as false. Scientific knowledge must validate every witness and testimony through personal experiment. Repeatable verification by experiment is crucial. The word of anyone, regardless of credentials, is worth nothing (no better than a fairytale or a lie) if it cannot be validated.

Through effective communication, humans obtain information or knowledge without conducting every experiment and enduring every experience. However, if someone believes that the only knowledge by which he should live is what he has personally obtained through experience and experiment, he rejects the use of communication for obtaining knowledge. If humans regarded science as the only means of obtaining knowledge, they would all die young.

Boiling pots are not hot until
every child burns his hand. Spoiled milk
is still good until every child is sick.
Vipers are friends until every child is
bitten. People can fly until every child

has jumped off a cliff. If we live only by science, we are all dead.

Education, media, government, and business are all structured on the reliability of communication. If every child needed to learn every mathematical proof and run every experiment to prove every scientific concept, they would never graduate and the public education system would be bankrupt. History class would be pointless because the only history that can be experienced is what is currently happening. Without communication, media would not exist. The only news people could know is the news they see happen in their own lives. Government, as slow at it is now, would come to a complete stop and the business world would return to a man with an ox and a plow. Science discovers truth for an individual; communication disseminates it to everyone else.

Effective Communication

Much of what humans consider fact is not what they have experienced, but what they have been told by a trusted source. Any time someone changes his behavior as a result of something he hears or reads, he assimilates a truth claim affirmed by another. For example, when someone yells "fire" and everyone starts for an exit, they trusted in the source and acted accordingly. They assimilated the truth claim that there was a fire. But people do not believe and assimilate everything everyone communicates to them. They can ignore or contest any communicated statement. Communication is only effective if the information communicated is assimilated by a receptor. Assimilation occurs most readily when the source is reliable, the truth claim is reasonable, and the receptor is willing to change.

Four attributes contribute to the reliability of a source: faithfulness, expertise, commitment, and motive.

Faithfulness develops through a relationship with time and experience as one individual evaluates the judgment, reasoning, consistency, and values of another.

Expertise is the qualification of an individual to make a truth claim about a certain subject. It is established through experience, study, and verification.

Commitment is an individual's willingness to stand behind a truth claim. If he claims something as truth, but behaves contrary or indifferent to that truth, the reality of the claimed truth is in question.

Motive is the reasons an individual promotes a truth claim. If that individual gains or benefits much from the assimilation of his truth claim by others, his reliability diminishes.

When an individual determines a source is reliable, he places his confidence and faith in that individual. Faith is not the ignorant acceptance of facts; faith is the acceptance of facts about a subject not experienced based on the reliability of the character of the information source. Faith is always based on the character and integrity of someone or something and results in a change of action or behavior.

When someone receives information through communication, they align and associate that information with whatever else they know about the subject. If the new information or truth claim is inconsistent with itself or with previously accepted truths, then it is questioned; the new truth claim or some previous truth claim will need to be rejected. If the new truth claim is to be accepted, then it will need to be further explained, verified by another source, or validated through experiment or experience. The more support there is for a truth claim and the more compatible it is with other truths, the more credible it is.

Since communication requires faith in the source, and since faith always results in a change of behavior, effective communication requires that the receptor be willing to change. An individual hesitates to accept information, regardless of the reliability of the communicator, if that information requires him to let go of something he values. However, if the information communicated by a reliable source warns of impending danger for something he values, then he assimilates the information much more readily. Effective communication depends on the reliability of the source and willingness of the receptor to change.

Relationships through Communication

People learn about each other through direct communication and by referral. Direct communication occurs when someone makes statements about himself attempting to convey who he is and what he values. Referrals occur when one individual testifies as a witness of the character of someone else. Referrals take many forms, including a formal job reference letter and a simple informal introduction. Relationships often begin with referrals. In direct communication, when two people first meet, the receptor has little by which to judge the reliability of the source since he knows nothing of the faithfulness, expertise, commitment, and motives of the communicator. However, with referrals, the receptor can begin the relationship based on his relationship with the reference. Because the receptor trusts the reference and the reference trusts the person being referred, the receptor is more likely to trust the referred individual. If the receptor does not know the reference, then the referral is of little value.

The power of referral can be seen in the role parents play in the lives of their children. A child will often believe something or trust someone simply because of a truth claim or referral of a parent. A child knows the character, values, and motives of his parents, since as the child has experienced his parents' love; he has learned to trust his parents. Because of this parent/child relationship, his parents become trusted sources of truth in his life. The child will believe and trust many things based on the confidence he has in his parents.

Relationships may begin with a combination of interaction and direct communication, although not as easily or as quickly as when initiated as by referral. This is true for establishing relationships between God and people. If God communicated directly with an individual, it would appear to be either a voice coming from nothing or from someone claiming to be God. Many people dismiss such things as dreams or illusions of the mind. Unless an individual is searching for God and willing to accept direct communication from God, he likely would not accept the claims of a strange voice. In a world without audio devices, a voice out of nowhere would be much more convincing and much more difficult to explain away. Today, however; a similar event may be discounted as a practical joke. If some reliable witness were to testify of the character, desire, actions, or statements of God on his behalf, it is much more likely that others would accept that testimony than if a voice from the sky were to make strange truth claims.

Without some communication, the God of the universe cannot establish eternal relationships with humans. So the debate is not whether God has communicated to humans, but what has he communicated to humans. In addition to creation and conscience, there are three primary ways in which God may communicate to individuals: direct revelation, authorship of a holy book, and testimony of those who have experienced God. When presented by information from any of these types of sources, people must evaluate its reliability.

Determining the Truth

The plentitude of gods presented by individuals, religions, and holy books create great difficulty in determining the constitution and character of God through the means of indirect communication. This multiplicity of proposed gods frequently gives rise to two questions "Why should I believe anyone?" and "How do I know who to believe?"

Why should I believe anyone? If multitudes of differing views abound and most of them are wrong, then the chance of believing a lie is high; so why bother go through so much angst only to settle on a wrong answer in the end? Why not just believe nothing? The person closest to believing nothing says "I don't know". However, someone cannot passively remain in such a state and believe nothing. If someone says "I don't know," then they need to either search for the answer or believe that the answer to God's existence and character is unimportant. If an individual admits he does not know God; does not know if God exists; or does not know if this is an important topic, then the presence of so many who declare there is important consequential truth that can be learned should result in the individual making an active search for the truth about God. The existence of the physical universe declares there is a creator; the constitution of the human declares the importance of knowing that creator. The view that there is no God or that knowing God is unimportant is a belief contrary to evidence.

How do I know who to believe? There are two ways in which someone's presentation of God can be evaluated: consistency of character and consistency with experience. When evaluating the proposed character of God by consistency of character, one must evaluate whether the proposed God can achieve his goals without violating his character. Goals are set by desires; desires are set by character. The goals of an individual must be consistent with his character. If a proposed God has a character which cannot realize his prescribed goals, this is evidence of a false God concept. Furthermore, the complexity of a human's experience should be consistent with his understanding of God. The attributes that one assigns to the nonphysical agent who created the physical universe should permit the possibility of the present universe as it currently exists. If the God of one's imagination would never permit the world of one's own experience to exist, then he is not the God that created the world which one experiences. *A proposed God must be able to take the universe from nothing to his end goal, passing through the universe as it exists today, without violating his own character.*

Many who try to prove the reality of their proposed God rely on positive identification. They claim that their God has conducted some supernatural act which has proven he is the true God whom they should worship. While this may function as evidence for that individual, it cannot serve as evidence for others. God can reveal himself to an individual by degrees and signs; but a person cannot rely on unexplainable events if his proposed God fails to meet the tests of consistency of character and experience. In a world of uncertainties and unknowns, everything must be scrutinized.

Silence

But if the heavens are silent, perhaps God is dead. Or perhaps he has lost interest or has given up hope. Or perhaps he is waiting for someone to search for him. If a man finds a body lying on the ground, he does not say to the body, "You are dead" and walk away. Nor does he ignore the body and assume it has lost interest in life. No, he understands his responsibility to determine if there is life. He asks, "Can you hear me?" He does whatever he can to get a response through touch, speech, CPR, or a defibrillator. Once all efforts have failed and no pulse having been found, the body is declared dead.

Some gleefully celebrate the silence of God in their life and fail to recognize their own failure of responsibility; they have not sought after God. Effective communication requires both a communicator and a willing receptor. If an individual has no interest in knowing God and refuses any suggestion of conforming his values or desires to those of another, there is little or no hope of God effectively communicating with him directly or by referral. The individual is content to believe a lie. Unless he sees the inconsistencies or failings of his own beliefs with the world he experiences, God can only reveal himself to that person by forcibly impresses upon them God's character in judgment resulting forever in a lost relationship.

If someone does recognize his responsibility and begins a meaningful search for God, he only needs to call out to God with the expectation of a response. When the time is right and the soul is ready, God will make himself known. Sometimes he speaks directly; often he uses his holy book; frequently he uses a personal reference. Those who come to know God and allow their lives to be conformed by God enjoy a relationship with God. God uses those people to testify of himself to others.

8 What is the Holy Bible?

The preceding chapter concludes the investigation into God through the study of the physical universe and the human experience. The remaining chapters of this book will evaluate how the teachings of the Holy Bible compare that which is revealed through the physical universe.

The Holy Bible is a letter from God to the world to communicate to people God's character, desires, and values. His purpose is that people might come to know him (1 John 1:1-3, Micah 6:8). To present the breadth and depth of God's character, the Holy Bible includes accounts of God's interactions and dealings with people, songs concerning God's character and notable deeds, and direct messages from God given to witnesses revealing his desires, laws, and future plans. God also explains through the Holy Bible how people can learn more about him, meet him, and develop a relationship with him.

When studying the Holy Bible, people ought to ask, "Is the God that the Holy Bible presents, the God that exists and that created the universe?" Through historical evidence, many have shown the reliability of the Holy Bible, but there is another test by which the Holy Bible must be evaluated: is the Holy Bible's portrayal of God consistent with the universe's portrayal of God? The Holy Bible must substantiate what God has revealed of himself through the creation of the physical universe.

Even the suggestion that the Holy Bible might be true draws the shouts and jeers of scoffers. Scoffers and fools have no interest in learning about God, but through scorn they desire to appear wise. They shout over everyone else and give no room for discussion or investigation. Such people are never helpful for discovering truth, for they refuse any suggestion that they might be wrong. A search for God requires patience, diligence, humility, and a desire to know the truth.

Throughout the following chapters, there are Bible verse references. The first part of the reference is the book of the Holy Bible in which the reference is found. The Holy Bible is divided into two parts: the Old Testament, which is composed of 39 different books; and the New Testament, which is composed of 27 difference books. The following part of the reference is the chapter of the book. The final part is the verse(s) of the chapter from which the reference is taken.

Book of the Holy Bible

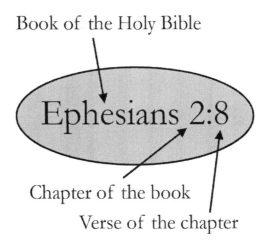

Chapter of the book

Verse of the chapter

(Key Bible passages are included
at the end of each chapter)

9   Who is God?

God as the Creator

In the Holy Bible, God is first introduced as the creator of the heavens, earth, and all life on earth (Genesis 1). This most fundamental attribute of God is reiterated throughout the Holy Bible. At the end of the Holy Bible, God is described as he "who created heaven and the things that are in them, and the earth and the things that are in it, and the sea and the things that are in it" (Revelation 10:6, MEV). God's act of creating the heavens and the earth was more than a child playing in a sand box or a blacksmith forging a tool. Psalm 104:1-5 speaks of God's stretching out the heavens and building the structure of the earth. John 1:3 says, "All things were created through Him, and without Him nothing was created that was created." God did not play with what already existed or just create some part within the physical universe. No, God created it all from nothing through his power and wisdom. Hebrews 11:3 defines what the Holy Bible teaches regarding God and the physical universe, "the universe was framed by the word of God, so that things that are seen were not made out of things which are visible."

In Job 38, God challenges Job's wisdom, knowledge, and power, and compares it to his own. "Where were you when I laid the foundations of the earth?" "To what are its foundations fastened?" "Have you commanded the morning in your days?" "Where is the path where light dwells? And as for darkness, where is its place?" "Have you entered the treasuries of the snow? Or have you seen the treasuries of the hail?" "Do you know the ordinances of heaven?" No one can compare with the wisdom and power of God as displayed in creation.

The Holy Bible places the essence of God outside of the physical universe. For God to create the entire physical universe, he himself must not be physical. At the time of creation, Genesis 1:2 introduces the Spirit of God, a nonphysical being. John 4:24 concurs and defines God as spirit. Being a spirit does not limit God from interacting with the physical by physical means or from representing himself in some physical form. What the Holy Bible does in defining God as a spirit is to attribute to him the ability to exist before the physical world, exist without a beginning, and exist without dependence on anything else. 1 Timothy 1:17 captures this essence of God, "Now to the eternal, immortal, invisible King, the only wise God, be honor and glory forever. Amen."

Furthermore, the Holy Bible is emphatic that the God of creation has ultimate power and authority. He is not a pawn in the service of some other god. In the prophesy to Isaiah, God declares "I am the first, and I am the last; besides Me there is no God" (Isaiah 44:6). In recounting the story of God and Abraham, the book of Hebrews also elevates God above all others, "For when God made a promise to Abraham, because He could vow by no one greater, He vowed by Himself" (Hebrews 6:13). Jesus Christ, in his prayer to God, also states the reality of there being only one God, "This is eternal life: that they may know You, the only true God" (John 17:3). King David, while appreciating who God was, sang, "I will be glad and rejoice in You; I will sing praise to Your name, O Most High" (Psalm 9:2). The Holy Bible leaves no doubt that the God it presents is the nonphysical agent that created the physical universe by his own power and authority.

A Unified God

There are those who find difficulty with the Holy Bible's presentation in the New Testament of God as the Father, the Son, and the Holy Spirit. They suppose that this means there are three Gods, which is inconsistent with the Old Testament teaching that there is only one God. The reader should recall the conclusion of the second chapter regarding the Consortium of the Gods. It is possible for multiple persons to be one God if they are in complete unity. The fusing of united beings into one will always happen anytime there is complete unity. As also concluded in the second chapter, the only manner in which unified beings can be distinguished from each other is in their spheres of authority and responsibility.

This concept of the unification of multiple elements in one can be related to a cube. There are three dimensions in a cube: height, width, and depth. For the existence of the cube, all three dimensions must be expressed. If one of them does not exist, regardless of the presence of the other two, the cube cannot exist. Each of the three dimensions has a role it must fulfill for the cube to exist. Furthermore, for the object to be a cube, each of the dimensions must be of equal length. If one dimension expresses dominance over the other two, then it is no longer a cube; it becomes a rectangular prism. For a cube to exist, there must be three equal, distinct dimensions unified into one object.

The Holy Bible defines God using the Father, the Son, and the Holy Spirit similar to how a cube is defined using three dimensions. The three dimensions, or persons, of God are unified with the same character, goals, and desires; yet are distinguishable by the offices or responsibilities they possess. There are a number of examples in the Holy Bible of the unity of the persons of God, including the act of creating the universe, the entering of God into the world, and the resurrection of Jesus Christ. In each of these examples, God is unified in desire and goal, but each person of God is identifiable by their role.

God the Father fills the place of authority. In Hebrews 1:1-2, the Father is seen creating the worlds through the Son and appointing the Son heir over creation. With authority, the Father sent the Son to be the savior of the world (John 12:49; 1 John 4:14). Furthermore, the power and authority of God was seen in the resurrection and exaltation of Jesus Christ, the Son of God (Ephesians 1:17-20).

The role of the Son of God is to reveal God to people. He is the image of God and the light. His first display of God to the world was through creation (Colossians 1:15-17; John 1:1-5, Romans 1:20). He continued to teach people about God by coming into the world as a man (John 1:14; 12:46) and living a holy life. Perhaps his greatest display of God was in his death and resurrection (John 10:10, 11, 17-18). Throughout the Son of God's revelations to the world, he displayed the power, authority, love, and perfection of God.

The Holy Spirit's role is that of being the energy and power of God. It was the Holy Spirit who moved upon the waters at creation (Genesis 1:1-2). The conception of Jesus Christ was by the Holy Spirit (Matthew 1:18-20). Furthermore, it is by the power of the Spirit that life is given in resurrection (Romans 8:11; 1 Peter 3:18). The unity of God was also seen at the baptism of Jesus Christ, when the Son of God began his public ministry with the power of the Holy Spirit and authority of the Father. The Holy Spirit descended upon the Son of God and the Father declared, "You are My beloved Son. In You I am well pleased" (Luke 3:21-22; 4:14, 32, 36).

A Logical God

Genesis 1 also presents God as logical and understandable, which makes it possible to communicate with him and to know him. God said, "Let the earth produce vegetation" and the earth produced vegetation (Genesis 1:11, 12). Seven times in Genesis 1, God speaks a command and the physical responds accordingly. There was no uncertainty in God's will, word, or command. His words translated directly into the physical, logical universe. Seven times out of seven the physical universe responded in accordance to God's word. God said what he meant, and the physical reacted correctly to what he said. Logical beings always act according to their desires, while illogical beings may act contrary to their desires. God acted according to his desires. God's satisfaction in the response of the physical to his command is recorded six times, "God saw that it was good," and at the completion of his creation, "it was very good." When God interacts with the physical universe, he does so logically. He speaks from his character and creation responds accordingly. There is complete consistency between who God is, what he says and what he does.

God's design for creation showcases his value of order and logic. God divided, categorized, and named light and darkness, day and night, and heaven, earth, and sea. He also established a means of keeping time with the sun, moon, and stars. God continued establishing order as he created plants and animals each after their own kinds. There is nothing random or illogical about the God presented in Genesis 1. Because God is logical, he can be studied and understood through his words, actions, and creation.

Creation of People

In Genesis 1, the Holy Bible introduces the creation of humans and details the account in Genesis 2.

God's creation of humans differs from the rest of creation. When God created humans, he said, "Let us make man in our image, after our likeness" (Genesis 1:26). The rest of creation was made according to God's desire; but it differed in its character from God. Humans were actually created with the same character and constitution as God. God further differentiated humans from the rest of creation by giving humans authority over creation.

As Genesis 2 details the creation of Adam and Eve, the first two people, one can begin to understand the significance of God's creating humans after his own image and likeness. Regarding Adam, God says, "It is not good that the man should be alone. I will make him a helper suitable for him." "Out of the ground the LORD God formed every beast of the field and every bird of the sky, and brought them to the man to see what he would call them … but for Adam there was not found a helper suitable for him." (Genesis 2:18-20). Afterward, God created a woman, Eve, from Adam's rib and brought her to Adam. It seems strange that God did not simply create two humans and put them together. Instead, he went through this process to teach an important lesson.

God designed and created Adam after God's character; and God said it was not good for Adam to be alone. God evaluated all the rest of creation which was designed after a different kind (its own kind) and determined that there was no suitable companion for Adam. Then God created another from Adam of the same kind as Adam to be a suitable companion for him. By comparison, it can be seen that if God was to have a companion, it must be of the same kind as God. By recording the details of the creation of Adam and Eve, the Holy Bible shows that God's motivation for creating humans was the desire for relationship. Love motivated God to create humans.

Some definition needs to be given to the idea that God created humans in his own image and likeness. The physical body came from dust and will return to dust (Genesis 2:7; 3:19), so it is not the physical body to which God is referring when he said he would make humans in his image and likeness. This image and likeness can be summed up in the idea of an origin– the ability and desire to create, relate, and define one's own character.

By forming Adam from the dust of the ground, God gave him a physical body; by breathing into his nostrils the breath of life, God made him an origin, "a living being" (Genesis 2:7). In so doing, God created a being who is responsible to God for his own action and for whatever is done in his body. As evidence of this, God instructed Adam and Eve to "Be fruitful and multiply, and replenish the earth and subdue it. Rule over the fish of the sea and over the birds of the air and over every living thing that moves on the earth" (Genesis 1:28). Because they were physical beings and had instruction from God, they were responsible to God. In addition, by having been given this instruction from God, they were given purpose and value. Genesis 1 and 2 are a beautiful display of God's character and desires, culminating in the creation of the first man and woman. It is consistent with what is seen in the world.

Key Bible Passages
(Modern English Version)

Genesis 1:1 In the beginning God created the heavens and the earth.

Genesis 1:27-28 So God created man in His own image; in the image of God He created him; male and female He created them. God blessed them and said to them, "Be fruitful and multiply, and replenish the earth and subdue it. Rule over the fish of the sea and over the birds of the air and over every living thing that moves on the earth."

Genesis 2:7 Then the Lord God formed man from the dust of the ground and breathed into his nostrils the breath of life, and man became a living being.

Luke 3:21-22 Now when all the people were baptized, and when Jesus also had been baptized and was praying, the heavens were opened, and the Holy Spirit descended in a bodily form like a dove on Him, and a voice came from heaven which said, "You are My beloved Son. In You I am well pleased."

John 1:14 The Word became flesh and dwelt among us, and we saw His glory, the glory as the only Son of the Father, full of grace and truth.

John 4:24 God is Spirit, and those who worship Him must worship Him in spirit and truth.

John 17:3 This is eternal life: that they may know You, the only true God, and Jesus Christ, whom You have sent.

1 Timothy 1:17 Now to the eternal, immortal, invisible King, the only wise God, be honor and glory forever. Amen.

Colossians 1:15-17 He is the image of the invisible God and the firstborn of every creature. For by Him all things were created that are in heaven and that are in earth, visible and invisible, whether they are thrones, or dominions, or principalities, or powers. All things were created by Him and for Him. He is before all things, and in Him all things hold together.

Hebrews 1:1-2 God, who at various times and in diverse ways spoke long ago to the fathers through the prophets, has in these last days spoken to us by His Son, whom He has appointed heir of all things, and through whom He made the world.

1 Peter 3:18 For Christ also has once suffered for sins, the just for the unjust, so that He might bring us to God, being put to death in the flesh, but made alive by the Spirit,

1 John 4:14 And we have seen and testify that the Father sent the Son to be the Savior of the world

10   Why is the world not perfect?

Paradise at Creation

The Holy Bible describes the world when God created it as "very good" (Genesis 1:31 MEV). It would be a most egregious lie to describe the world today as very good. The first few chapters of Genesis outline the path the world took to reach its current state. Before investigating the cause of the devastation in the world, it is important to understand the original conditions and design. Study of the initial design throws light on God's intentions, plans, and goals for the future.

Paradise would have been a fitting description of the universe when God created it. The death, destruction, suffering, and disaster experienced today did not infect the earth at its beginning. At creation, the earth was vastly different than it is today. Genesis

107

describes an earth where all creatures were vegetarians (Genesis 1:30); and where the ground was watered by the dew because it did not rain (Genesis 2:5). The world into which Adam and Eve were brought knew nothing of the turmoil of the present one. The world, when first created, was a place of peace.

God created Adam, placed him in the Garden of Eden, and gave him responsibility for taking care of the garden (Genesis 2:15). He had full responsibility. If the garden was neglected, fell into disorder, and became overgrown, Adam was accountable. If it grew into a beautiful and productive garden, he could take credit. God also gave a commandment to Adam: he could eat the fruit of every tree in the garden except for one, the Tree of the Knowledge of Good and Evil. If he did eat of it, on that day, he would be placed under the curse and punishment of death (Genesis 2:16-17; 3:19).

After God created a perfect world for Adam and Eve to live, it may seem foolish that God created an opportunity for disobedience, death, and sorrow to disrupt that paradise. However, God's priority was not a satisfying, peaceful, physical life; God's priority was to establish love relationships with people. Such relationships require both faith and love. Faith is expressed through confidence in a promise or obedience to a commandment; love is expressed through sacrifice. In a place of perfection, where all needs are met and people can do whatever they desire, there is no opportunity for true relationships to be formed or developed. When God commanded Adam not to eat of a certain tree in the garden, he assigned a punishment for disobedience. Thus, Adam and Eve were given an opportunity to demonstrate their faith in God's word and make a willful sacrifice of an experience for the sake of their relationship with God. When Adam and Eve ultimately broke God's commandment (Genesis 3:6), it was evidence that they did not possess or value their relationship with God. Eve doubted God's word; Adam willingly disobeyed it (Genesis 3:1-6).

At the simplest level, the Tree of the Knowledge of Good and Evil was a test of priorities, love, and faith for Adam and Eve. Obedience or disobedience to God's commandment was the true test of their relationship. However, the Tree of the Knowledge of Good and Evil goes beyond being a simple test; for in it is the beginning of the solution to the resulting consequences. In their initial condition, Adam and Eve had no need to judge between good and evil; they only needed to depend on God for direction and guidance. Their lack of a moral conscience is evident in three ways. First, Adam and Eve did not know instinctively that they should not eat fruit of the Tree of the Knowledge of Good and Evil; God had to give a direct command. Second, Genesis 2:25 says, "they were both

naked, the man and his wife, and were not ashamed."
They had no understanding of shame or of right and
wrong. Third, when Eve was tempted, part of what
enticed her was the possibility of being made wise,
knowing good and evil (Genesis 3:5,6). She recognized
that they did not have the wisdom of God to know
good and evil.

When Adam and Eve chose to disobey God,
they displayed distrust and disregard for the word,
wisdom, guidance, and motives of God. They forsook
the counsel of God and would have gone their own way
in ignorance, never to develop a relationship with God.
But, the tree from which they were commanded not to
eat bestowed the knowledge of good and evil. Although
it was disobedience, when Adam and Eve ate of that
tree they gained a conscience. The conscience of each
individual helps them decide what they ought to do and
ought not to do. The conscience gives the ability to
evaluate the desires of another person and determine if
their own desires are compatible. Using God as the
standard of righteousness, Adam and Eve could
determine right and wrong- good and evil. The
capacities gained through the conscience permitted
repentance and a way for Adam and Eve to obtain a
relationship with God.

God's decision that death would be the
consequence for breaking his commandment was not

haphazard or extreme. Death maintains God as the ultimate deity of the universe, establishes a check and balance against evil, and gives humans a need to return to God. God does not desire death to be part of his creation, just as he did not desire Adam and Eve to disobey him. But God does use death to gain what disobedience destroys: relationship. But death will not always reign; it is not the culmination of God's creation. That is proven by the existence of another particular tree God had placed in the Garden of Eden.

Along with the Tree of the Knowledge of Good and Evil, God created the Tree of Life. Both were placed in the Garden of Eden. In the beginning of Genesis, the Tree of Life seems to serve no purpose. Before Adam and Eve sinned, they had no need of it, for they would not die. After they sinned and were cursed to die, they were driven out of the garden and had no opportunity to eat of the Tree of Life (Genesis 3:22-24). However, the purpose of the Tree of Life is found at the end of the Holy Bible. In the future, when God is worshipped and evil is defeated, the Tree of Life "bore twelve fruits, each tree yielding its fruit every month. The leaves of the tree were for the healing of the nations" (Revelation 22:2). The presence of the Tree of Life in the Garden of Eden proves that God's ultimate plan for the world extends far beyond the paradise of the Garden of Eden. The Tree of Life also testifies that

God is able to abolish death and give eternal life. There is a future when "God will wipe away every tear from their eyes; there shall be no more death, nor sorrow, nor crying. There shall be no more pain" (Revelation 21:4). Anyone desiring eternal life can turn to God and have confidence that he will give life.

That Serpent of Old, the Devil, and Satan

Genesis 3:1 introduces one more aspect of the Garden of Eden which needs explanation. When Adam and Eve disobeyed God, they were responsible for their actions. God created a perfect world, gave Adam responsibility for it, and Adam brought death into the world through his disobedience and sin (Romans 5:12). Therefore, Adam bears the responsibility for a ruined world. However, Genesis 3:1 introduces the serpent, a creature so apparently inconsistent with the rest of God's creation. The serpent was subtle, deceptive, manipulative, and full of lies. How could it have been part of creation if creation was so perfect? The answer is found in the last book of the Holy Bible, Revelation, where twice it refers to Satan as "that Serpent of Old" (Revelation 12:9; 20:2). Satan is also given responsibility for the actions and lies of the serpent: "He was a murderer from the beginning, and does not stand in the truth, because there is no truth in him. When he speaks a lie, he speaks from his own resources, for he is a liar and the father of it." (John 8:44). The physical serpent was a creature that God created, but Satan possessed that serpent and used it as a tool to disrupt God's creation. The Holy Bible speaks of similar demon possession a number of times (Matthew 9:32; 12:22, Mark 5:15; 7:26, Luke 9:42, John 13:27).

Satan was originally an angel who was perfect and had been given authority over other angels. But he was prideful, so he lost his place of privilege and responsibility (Ezekiel 28:14-17, Revelation 12:7-9, 1 Timothy 3:6). After Satan sinned and was punished, he became a bitter enemy of God, seeking to destroy all that is good (1 Peter 5:8, John 8:44, Hebrews 2:14, Acts 13:10). God could have banished Satan forever from his presence, but instead, God permitted Satan to wage war and attack God's creation. In his rebellion against God, Satan robbed God of glory, honor, and some of his angels, and disturbed and defiled that which was perfect. God could have destroyed Satan and been done with him, but God had a greater plan. Instead of cutting his losses and moving on, God chose to turn the rebellion and hatred of Satan into even greater good. In the Garden of Eden, Satan's aim was to destroy paradise; but through Satan's rebellion, God created world conditions in which he could obtain eternal relationships. Satan seems to have accomplished his goal of wreaking havoc in the world, but God has not completed his work—the Tree of Life has yet to be unveiled. God will have the final victory. Through Satan's rebellion, God will gain more than Satan has destroyed.

In the Garden of Eden, Satan, the tempter, functioned as a catalyst. He brought Eve's attention to the Tree of the Knowledge of Good and Evil and put the seed of doubt into her mind. Once Eve had eaten of the fruit, she offered it to Adam, who also ate it (Genesis 3:1-6). Adam was not deceived; he willingly made his choice, knowing the consequences of his actions (1 Timothy 2:14). Both Adam and Eve failed because of their lack of relationship with God. Eve did not have faith in God; Adam did not have love for God. Eve trusted the serpent and Adam placed a relationship with Eve ahead of a relationship with God.

The disobedience of Adam and Eve bound them under the curse of death; however, death was not the only result. As a result of their disobedience, there would be pain in childbirth and the ground would be cursed with thorns and thistles. These consequences would serve as continuous reminders of their sin, and as a testimony to future generations of the results of disobeying God, rather than trusting him.

Through Adam and Eve's failure, God had further opportunity to reveal his character. As when

Satan rebelled, God did not banish Adam and Eve from his presence forever and move on with some other project. Having created Adam and Eve, God knew what they would do because he knew their character. Their sin did not surprise God. Self-will, lust, and pride are inherent to beings. Love, humility, and relationships develop over time, so God was prepared to continue working with Adam and Eve, gradually revealing himself to them and developing a relationship with them. God had promised that Adam and Eve would die physically because of their sin and so they did. But God still cared about them, loved them, and did not forsake them. In a symbolic, prophetic act of love, God killed an animal to provide clothes for Adam and Eve (Genesis 3:21).

The corruption of a perfect world which has descended into the abyss of the present began when Adam and Eve chose to disobey God; however, that was only the beginning. A few generations after Adam, the world had transformed into a cesspool of immorality as people ignored their conscience, God, and Noah, a preacher of righteousness (Genesis 6:5, 2 Peter 2:5). God brought judgment upon them by breaking up the deeps and pouring down the rain, completely flooding the earth (Genesis 6:13; 7:11, 12). As a result, the surface of the earth was fragmented; the atmosphere completely changed; and the world became an ongoing natural disaster; yet the corruption did not stop. God commanded the generations after the flood to multiply and fill the earth (Genesis 9:1), but they rejected God and built a city and tower to glorify themselves (Genesis 11:4). God then judged mankind again, disrupting their actions by causing them to be unable to communicate with one another through confusion of language (Genesis 11:5-8). So it has continued; as people reject and disobey God, the world becomes even more distant from the paradise it once was.

Key Bible Passages
(Modern English Version)

Genesis 2:15-17 Then the LORD God took the man and put him in the garden of Eden to tend and keep it. And the LORD God commanded the man, saying, "Of every tree of the garden you may freely eat; but of the tree of the knowledge of good and evil you shall not eat, for in the day that you eat of it you shall surely die."

Genesis 3: 4-6 Then the serpent said to the woman, "You will not surely die. For God knows that in the day you eat of it your eyes will be opened, and you will be like God, knowing good and evil."So when the woman saw that the tree was good for food, that it was pleasant to the eyes, and a tree desirable to make one wise, she took of its fruit and ate. She also gave to her husband with her, and he ate.

Genesis 6:13 And God said to Noah, "The end of all flesh has come before Me, for the earth is filled with violence through them; and behold, I will destroy them with the earth.

Genesis 9:1 So God blessed Noah and his sons, and said to them: "Be fruitful and multiply, and fill the earth.

Genesis 11:4-8 And they said, "Come, let us build ourselves a city, and a tower whose top is in the heavens; let us make a name for ourselves, lest we be scattered abroad over the face of the whole earth."But the LORD came down to see the city and the tower which the sons of men had built. And the LORD said, "Indeed the people are one and they all have one language, and this is what they begin to do; now nothing that they propose to do will be withheld from them. Come, let Us go down and there confuse their language, that they may not understand one another's speech." So the LORD scattered them abroad from there over the face of all the earth, and they ceased building the city.

Romans 5:12 Therefore, just as through one man sin entered the world, and death through sin, and thus death spread to all men, because all sinned

11 How does God communicate with people?

The Foundation of Faith

The history of the world is little more than misery, sorrow, and death; but as the skies grow darker, the hope of the Tree of Life grows brighter. With the passing of generations, God continues to reveal more of himself and more of his plan for the redemption of the world.

Faith is the key to return to God, for it is faith that establishes relationship. Had Adam and Eve had faith in God, they would never have disobeyed God by eating of the fruit of the Tree of Knowledge of Good and Evil. Despite their disobedience, God still wanted a relationship with Adam and Eve; this was evident from his provision of clothes for them. But to have that relationship, Adam and Eve needed to have faith in God. The same is true throughout the history of the world.

Hebrews 11 outlines a long history of those who had faith in God. The list begins with Abel, a son of Adam. Abel's faith is linked to his willingness to give to God that which was best. Five generations after Abel, Enoch is also identified for his faith. Enoch "pleased God. And without faith it is impossible to please God, for he who comes to God must believe that He exists and that He is a rewarder of those who diligently seek Him" (Hebrews 11:5-6, MEV). Noah "became an heir of the righteousness that comes by faith" (Hebrews 11:7). Abraham, Isaac, Jacob, and Joseph are all listed for having faith in the promises of God. Moses as well had faith in God "choosing rather to suffer affliction with the people of God than to enjoy the pleasures of sin for a time" (Hebrews 11:24-25). The list in Hebrews 11 of people who had faith in God continues on, covering many of the people recorded in the Old Testament of the Holy Bible.

Throughout time, faith has brought people into a relationship with God. Sadly, the general characteristic of many generations has not been faith in God, but a misplaced or misdirected faith in something or someone else. The Holy Bible chronicles over and over how people placed their faith in something other than God. They forgot about God and attempted to satisfy their own lusts and pride. As a result, God judged them and revealed the error of their ways. At such times, the judgment and punishment of God served as an indicator of the need for repentance, as well as an example for others. God's actions always reveal some aspect of his character and bring his creation back towards alignment with his character and purposes.

The Flood

From the time of expulsion from the Garden of Eden to the flooding of the whole earth, the general human attitude developed into a faith in self. The result was that "the wickedness of man was great on the earth, and that every intent of the thoughts of his heart was continually only evil" (Genesis 6:5). God had given people a conscience and they had the history of God's judgment of Adam and Eve, but still they chose to fulfill the lusts of their flesh rather than trust in God. As a result, God flooded the whole earth, saving only Noah and his family. "Noah was a just man and blameless among his contemporaries. Noah walked with God" (Genesis 6:9). In God's dealings with the world in Noah's day, several principles of God are highlighted. God is patient and merciful, but he will act in judgment when he can bear wickedness no longer. God deals in judgment not only with individuals, but also with whole groups or systems. When a system such as a culture, nation, or generation has turned against God and is vile in his sight, he brings judgment upon the whole system, declaring his hatred of it. When this happens, everything functioning within the system or representing the system is destroyed. Throughout the Old Testament, God is recorded as doing this with the world (Genesis 6:7), nations (Deuteronomy 7:1-2; 9:1-6; 20:16-18, Hebrews 11:31) and cities (Genesis 18:20-21; 19:24-25).

This physical destruction of earthly systems is not the same as personal eternal judgment. The physical judgment of systems results in physical eradication from the world; but God will deal individually with all those killed in the destruction of the system. God's wrath and judgment on a system does not imply wrath on every individual within a system, although there will be wrath for the majority. God is able to save the righteous and innocent (Isaiah 57:1-2, Genesis 18:22-32). They may have lost their lives in the destruction of the system, but their souls are with God; that is of much greater value.

The Tower of Babel

After the great flood, God made a covenant with Noah and his family and gave them a commandment to "Be fruitful and multiply and fill the earth" (Genesis 9:1). God also promised that he would never destroy the world again with a flood and used the rainbow as a sign of this promise (Genesis 9:11-16). However, the rainbow is also a reminder that God does judge the wicked.

A few generations after the flood, people turned away from God again. Despite having a conscience, the history of Adam's time and Noah's time, the reminder of the rainbow, and the commandment of God, they gave way to their pride. Rather than trusting in God as they spread out upon the earth and filled it, they placed their faith in civilization and agreed to live together in a city and make a name for themselves (Genesis 11:4). They did the same thing as Noah's generation; turning from God, they placed their faith in something less than God. Noah's generation attempted to set their own destiny without God, but God showed them they were weak before him. In the generation of Babel, they trusted in the protection of their civilization. They tried living without God, but God did not permit that. He confused their language, causing their civilization to fall apart and disperse over the earth in fulfillment of God's command (Genesis 11:7, 8).

Israel – God's Nation

After the confusion of language, people recognized the existence and need for a supernatural being. Unfortunately, due to the influence of pride and lust, they invented gods of their own imagination. They attributed false characteristics to God that would permit their own ungodly desires. The nations of the world established national gods whom they worshipped, trusted, and on whom they depended to provide for them and protect them from their enemies.

From out of this system of false national gods, God chose to form a nation to which he would reveal himself so it could represent him and demonstrate to the rest of the world who the true God is. The nation began with Abraham (Genesis 12:1-3), and with each generation, God revealed more about himself. The history of God's formation of the nation of Israel is fascinating in all its detail, as recorded in the first five books of the Holy Bible.

God's goal for Israel was that through them the rest of the nations of the world would recognize their sin and learn who the real God was, and thus, desire to trust in him, rather than the gods of their own imaginations (Genesis 12:1-3, Exodus 14:18, Joshua 2:8-11). Those nations that chose to worship their own gods and ignore the only true God came under God's judgment (Deuteronomy 9:4; 31:11-13).

In a great display of power and might, God devastated the land of Egypt where the Israelites had been slaves. Then he brought them into the land of Canaan, which he had promised to give to Abraham's descendants (Genesis 12:6-7, Exodus 10:7, Joshua 2:8-11). Through the Israelites journey from Egypt to Canaan, God established a covenant of laws and promises with them, detailing his character and desires. Afterward, God brought Israel into Canaan and began destroying the nations that lived there. Similar to the manner in which God judged the world in Noah's time, God ordered the destruction of many of these nations. While God would later have personal dealings with each individual regarding their eternal state, God used the destruction of those nations to testify that their sins and false gods were an abomination to the true God. God had been merciful, having given those nations many generations to repent (Genesis 15:16, 18); but the time of their judgment had come. Using the nation of Israel as the executioner, God dealt with those nations (Deuteronomy 7:1-4).

God used Israel not only as an executioner to deliver punishment to the surrounding nations and their false gods, but also as an example for the remaining nations. As he outlined in his covenant with Israel, to which they had agreed, God blessed Israel when they followed him, and punished Israel when they forgot him and worshipped the gods of the nations (Deuteronomy 11:26-28). A cycle of turning away from God and being restored back to God through judgment is repeated throughout Israel's history as recorded in the Old Testament.

The Old Testament closes with the nation of Israel in terrible condition. Because of their rejection of the true God and their worship of false gods, God permitted most of the nation to be taken into slavery by various other nations. Some were able to return to their homeland and rebuild, but Israel never again rose to the height of power and glory it once possessed. Presently Israel waits for a promised King, a Messiah, who will restore Israel and the world to glory and peace.

God speaking today

God continues to testify of himself in the present generation. Creation testifies of his existence, power, and authority (Romans 1:20). The conscience continues to work within people, pushing them to realize that something is wrong with their desires and actions (Romans 2:14-15). The history of all that God has done continues to be told, teaching people of the character and behavior of God. The continued existence of the Jews, descendants of Abraham, Isaac, and Jacob, against all odds, also bears witness that there is a God who keeps the promises he has made to the nation of Israel (Jeremiah 31:31-34). Finally, there are those who have turned to God and trusted him, who have been transformed and declare that there is a God who is mighty, just, righteous, merciful, and loving. (John 17:20-21, 1 Timothy 2:5-7, 2 Corinthians 5:19-21)

God is active and working today. He is laboring to bring people to himself in faith and love. To those who search for God, he will reveal himself. He will establish a relationship with all who are willing to let go of lust and pride, and instead trust in the character and love of God.

Key Bible Passages
(Modern English Version)

Genesis 12:1-3 Now the LORD said to Abram, "Go from your country, your family, and your father's house to the land that I will show you. I will make of you a great nation; I will bless you and make your name great, so that you will be a blessing. I will bless them who bless you and curse him who curses you, and in you all families of the earth will be blessed."

Deuteronomy 9:1, 4-5 Hear, O Israel! You are to cross over the Jordan today, to go in to possess nations greater and mightier than you, great cities fortified up to heaven, ... Do not say in your heart, after the LORD your God has driven them out before you, "On account of my righteousness the LORD has brought me in to possess this land," but it is because of the wickedness of these nations the LORD is driving them out before you. It is not because of your righteousness or the uprightness of your heart that you enter to possess their land, but because of the wickedness of these nations that the LORD your God drives them out before you, and that He may fulfill the word which the LORD swore to your fathers, Abraham, Isaac, and Jacob.

Deuteronomy 11:26-28 See, I am setting before you today a blessing and a curse: the blessing if you obey the commandments of the LORD your God, which I am commanding you today, and the curse, if you will not obey the commandments of the LORD your God, but turn from the way which I am commanding you today, to go after other gods which you have not known.

Deuteronomy 20:16-18 But of the cities of these people, which the LORD your God is giving you for an inheritance, you must not leave alive anything that breathes. But you shall completely destroy them: namely, the Hittites, and the Amorites, the Canaanites, and the Perizzites, the Hivites, and the Jebusites, just as the LORD your God has commanded you, so that they do not teach you to participate in all their abominations, which they have done to their gods, causing you to sin against the LORD your God.

2 Corinthians 5:20-21 So we are ambassadors for Christ, as though God were pleading through us. We implore you in Christ's stead: Be reconciled to God. God made Him who knew no sin to be sin for us, that we might become the righteousness of God in Him.

Romans 1:20 The invisible things about Him—His eternal power and deity—have been clearly seen since the creation of the world and are understood by the things that are made, so that they are without excuse.

Hebrews 11:6 And without faith it is impossible to please God, for he who comes to God must believe that He exists and that He is a rewarder of those who diligently seek Him.

12 How do we start a relationship with God?

God of Love

The character of God in all its detail and color is woven into the Holy Bible from beginning to end. Of all its different aspects and attributes, the feature of love is the most vibrant strand. It is seen in God's words and actions, his desires and motivations, through peace and war, in friendship and betrayal, during the day and the night, on mountains and in storms. God's love stands out against all else.

The Holy Bible begins its story of love at the creation of the world. During creation, God brought into existence a perfect system of life and beauty. The week culminated with God's creation of two people (designed and formed after God's own character) with whom God was able to have a relationship. More than

129

matter or dust, God breathed into Adam the breath of life and Adam became a living being (Genesis 2:7). With such an intimate act, the first human came to life.

Genesis 2-3 details the interaction between God and the first two humans, who, despite the blessings of God, chose to turn away from him. Yet God did not turn away from them, but continued to demonstrate his love in mercy and grace. God continued to express his love with each generation. God spoke with Cain (Genesis 4:9-10). He walked with Enoch (Genesis 5:22) and Noah (Genesis 6:9). He was a friend of Abraham (James 2:23). He spoke with Moses face to face (Exodus 33:11). He described David as a man after God's own heart (Acts 13:22). The Old Testament of the Bible details story after story of God's reaching out to people, loving them, and revealing himself to them. Perhaps the greatest love story in the Old Testament is that of God and the nation of Israel. It is so sad to read of God's great love shunned by the adulterous Israel (Ezekiel 16:25-28, Hosea 3:1, 6:10). Even so, God has not forsaken them. The New Testament follows the Old Testament, carrying on the theme of God's love.

Love is more than a nice characteristic of God. It is what motivates him. It permeates everything he does. All created things were created by God for his pleasure (Colossians 1:15-16). That which pleases God is love. This is manifested by the ultimate standard and purpose of God as expressed in the law and commandment that he has given. "You shall love the Lord your God with all your heart" (Luke 10:27 MEV). The greatest result of someone's knowing God and having a relationship with God is that they will love God and others (1 John 4:7-8). God does not just want to be loved, but wants those who love him to love others as well. "If you love Me, keep My commandments" (John 14:15). "A new commandment I give to you, that you love one another" (John 13:34).

However, rather than expressing love for God and others, humans, by nature, express love for self. Humans begin their existence as strangers to God; they do not know his character, desires, or behavior (Romans 3:11-12). They have never met him and have no relationship with him. Through creation (Romans 1:20), conscience (Romans 2:14-15), and witnesses (Romans 3:19-26), God reveals himself to each human so they might seek after a relationship with him. However, because human nature is to serve and delight self, conflict arises between every individual and God.

God's character is to love and serve others. For there to be a harmonious relationship between God and a human, the human needs a character compatible with God. To obtain such, they need to exchange their pride and lust for humility and love (Micah 6:8). This requires a complete change in character and desire, resulting in a complete change in behavior. This is repentance: a complete turning away and letting go of a past life and the embracing of a new one. God calls sinners to repentance (Matthew 9:13), desires that all repent (2 Peter 3:9), and rejoices when they do repent (Luke 15:7).

In Need of Redemption

Repentance aligns people's character with God's character. This sets the path for a future relationship; but before that relationship can be enjoyed, the past must be addressed. Sin is disobedience to God. It is the cause of the broken relationship between God and people (Isaiah 59:2). The Holy Bible is clear that all have sinned (Romans 3:23) and the punishment of sin is death (Romans 6:23). People's sin has brought them under the curse and punishment of the law. All who have sinned need to be redeemed from the curse of the law before they can have a relationship with God or they will be lost forever.

To be redeemed from the curse of the law, an individual must have a substitute who will bear the punishment of their sins. A substitute takes the place of condemnation for a sinner. This is illustrated throughout the Old Testament through the system of sacrifices given to the Nation of Israel (Leviticus 4-5). However, the Old Testament sacrifices were only a picture of God's plan for the salvation of souls from sin (Hebrews 10:1, 10-12). For the law to be satisfied and souls redeemed from the law, a willing human, without sin, must be the substitute (Hebrews 9:22-28, 1 Peter 2:21-24, 2 Corinthians 5:21). The only way for a human to live without sin is if they possess the same character and desires as God. A human would need to possess such character and desires from birth without going through the process of learning about God and repenting from a sinful life. Such a person would have to be God. For God to redeem people from the curse of the law, he had to enter the world as a human and die.

The New Testament books of Matthew and Luke both record how God entered the world as a human. "The angel answered [Mary], "The Holy Spirit will come upon you, and the power of the Highest will overshadow you. Therefore the Holy One who will be born will be called the Son of God." (Luke 1:35). "for He who is conceived in her is of the Holy Spirit. She will bear a Son, and you shall call His name JESUS, for He will save His people from their sins." (Matthew 1:20-21).

While it is implied that Jesus would have the character of God (for he was born of God), the four gospel accounts demonstrate this by detailing the holy, godly life of Jesus. An evaluation of his character and life is given by the Apostle Peter and Apostle Paul. "He committed no sin, nor was deceit found in His mouth" (1 Peter 2:22). "God made Him who knew no sin to be sin for us, that we might become the righteousness of God in Him" (2 Corinthians 5:21). The only way Jesus could live a perfect sinless life was to possess the character of God from his birth. Two other verses in the Holy Bible that speak to this are these: "who, being in the form of God, did not consider equality with God something to be grasped" (Philippians 2:6) and "God was revealed in the flesh" (1 Timothy 3:16). God became a human so that he might become a substitute, for there was no other suitable substitute.

In Jesus Christ, God provided a perfect substitute who is able to redeem repentant people from the curse of the law. To satisfy the law, Jesus died as a substitute. In John 10:10-17, Jesus speaks of coming to earth for the purpose of laying down his life so that others might live. Jesus Christ's death, recorded in each of the gospels (Matthew 27:50, Mark 15:37, Luke 23:46, John 19:30), accomplished all that sinners were unable to accomplish for their own redemption. Ephesians 1:7 describes the work and result of Jesus Christ's sacrifice, "In Him we have redemption through His blood and the forgiveness of sins according to the riches of His grace."

A sinner who dies under the curse of the law without a relationship with God is lost forever (Matthew 7:23). After death, they have no means of establishing a relationship with God and they have no power within themselves to come to life again. In death, Jesus Christ's case was quite different from that of an unrepentant sinner. First, while Jesus Christ died as a consequence of sin, but not his own sin (1 John 3:5), for he had never sinned (1 Peter 2:21-22). He always had a perfect relationship with God (John 10:30, John 8:29). Second, in death, because he is God, he had the power to bring himself to life again (John 10:18). Because Jesus Christ satisfied the law and pleased God, he did not remain dead. Instead, he rose victorious from the grave and was seen alive by many witnesses (1 Corinthians 15:3-8).

A God Who Forgives

By satisfying the demands of the law through the death of Jesus Christ, God purchased people who have repented, freeing them from the law (Ephesians 1:12-14) and gaining the right to forgive them (Colossians 1:14). Forgiveness, while it is unattainable through the law, is absolutely necessary for a relationship to exist after an offense has occurred. An offense implicates a break of trust or disagreement of values. It indicates the presence of a problem or point of contention, which causes disunity. The offense or disagreement must be remedied, or it will infect and destroy the whole relationship. The remedy begins with repentance, a realignment of values, and is completed with forgiveness. Forgiveness is a willingness to absorb the loss caused by the offender without exacting retribution. Forgiveness places the value of the relationship over the loss caused by the offense. If the loss is too great and forgiveness does not occur, then the relationship is lost as well.

Jesus Christ knew the importance of forgiveness in a relationship, and so commands his disciples to forgive their brethren if they repent (Luke 17:3-4). It is in God's character to forgive those who come to him in repentance. 1 John 1:9 highlights all these aspects of forgiveness. Speaking of those who have already been redeemed, it says, "If we confess our sins, He is faithful and just to forgive us our sins and cleanse us from all unrighteousness." Not only does God have the right to forgive sins, but he can be trusted to forgive the sins of the repentant.

Faith in God's Character

The Holy Bible says that Christ has died as a substitute and that God will forgive repentant sinners.

However, it is up to each individual whether or not they will trust in God to forgive. As John 3:16 states: "*Whosoever* believes in Him." Some people struggle with believing the Holy Bible because they are concerned about the possibility of the Holy Bible being corrupted and misinterpreted. This is an important concern, and in response to it, much research has been done which supports the historical validity and accuracy of the Holy Bible. These findings are presented in a number of apologetics books and have helped many people who were struggling to trust the teachings of the Holy Bible. However, faith in all the people who have compiled, preserved, and translated the Holy Bible is not the same as having faith in God to actually perform what he has promised. A relationship with God requires faith in the character of God, not faith in the skill of historians and archeologists. If an individual has faith in the character of the loving God who created the universe for the purpose of forming relationships with people, then they will believe two things: they will believe that God did or will provide a substitute to redeem them from the law; and that God will forgive repentant sinners and not reject those who trust in him. The Holy Bible presents the character, desires, and actions of God, and it is the individual's responsibility to decide whether or not they will trust in that God. The results of their decision are laid out in John 3:36 "He who believes in the Son has eternal life. He who does not believe the Son shall not see life, but the wrath of God remains on him."

Justified and Ready for Responsibility

With faith and redemption comes justification (Romans 3:23-24; 5:1, 9). Sinners have failed to meet God's standards and expectations. They have proven themselves untrustworthy and unable to protect and promote what God values. However, through repentance, a sinner's desires are changed; through faith, they establish that which they once violated: God and a relationship with him. Faith in someone comes from knowledge of that person and a willingness to depend upon that person. It lets go of self and pride, and embraces love and humility. A sinner acts against God out of pride and lust inhibiting a relationship with God, but enters into a relationship with God by turning to God in love and humility trusting in him to redeem and forgive.

The faith, love, and humility of a person towards God not only changes their values and actions, but allows the Spirit of God to transform them and produce the fruit of the Spirit within them (Galatians 5:16-25). A repentant sinner is also transformed by Jesus Christ's living in them as Paul testified of his own life experience in Galatians 2:20. All this by the power and design of

God transforms a sinner into a justified individual who is now able to protect and promote that which God values– a person whom God can trust with responsibility.

Full Redemption in the Future

One of those responsibilities is being a witness for God to others on earth: "ambassadors for Christ" (2 Corinthians 5:19-20, 1 Peter 3:15). That is why God leaves redeemed people in unredeemed physical bodies on an unredeemed earth (Romans 8:18-23, 1 Corinthians 15:42-54). Upon repentance and faith, God could immediately remove a justified person from the earth and take him to heaven. However, he chooses rather to show his confidence in the justified by giving him responsibility. This also gives the redeemed person the opportunity to demonstrate his faithfulness and love for God and the reality of justification. As with everything God chooses to do, the result is greater blessing for others as relationships deepen and more people enter into relationships with God (2 Corinthians 2:14, Romans 2:4; 8:27-28; 10:14-15; 12:2).

God has promised that in the future the physical bodies of the redeemed and the whole physical creation will be released from the curse of sin and will no longer suffer the effects of sin (1 Corinthians 15:54-57). Just as

Jesus Christ rose from the dead and ascended into the presence of God, so God will resurrect all who trust him and they will spend eternity with God (Romans 8:11, 1 Corinthians 15:52, Ephesians 1:20, 1 Thessalonians 1:10). A future day is coming when the earth will be rid of sin, death and Satan (Revelation 20:10, 21:1, 4). The Lord Jesus Christ will accomplish this when he returns to establish his kingdom on earth (1 Corinthians 15:20-26, Revelation 22:3-7). What happens after the redemption of the whole creation and the gathering of God's people unto himself is still in part a mystery, but it is assured that the relationships of God will continue to the blessing of the redeemed. The God who created the universe and relates to those who seek him will continue to create and relate for eternity.

Key Bible Passages
(Modern English Version)

Isaiah 59:2 But your iniquities have made a separation between you and your God, and your sins have hidden His face from you so that He will not hear.

Matthew 1:20-21 But while he thought on these things, the angel of the Lord appeared to him in a dream saying, "Joseph, son of David, do not be afraid to take Mary as your wife, for He who is conceived in her is of the Holy

Spirit. She will bear a Son, and you shall call His name JESUS, for He will save His people from their sins."

John 10:10-15 The thief does not come, except to steal and kill and destroy. I came that they may have life, and that they may have it more abundantly. "I am the good shepherd. The good shepherd lays down His life for the sheep. But he who is a hired hand, and not a shepherd, who does not own the sheep, sees the wolf coming, and leaves the sheep, and runs away. So the wolf catches the sheep and scatters them. The hired hand runs away because he is a hired hand and does not care about the sheep. "I am the good shepherd. I know My sheep and am known by My own. Even as the Father knows Me, so I know the Father. And I lay down My life for the sheep.

John 19:30 When Jesus had received the sour wine, He said, "It is finished." And He bowed His head and gave up His spirit.

Romans 3:23 For all have sinned and come short of the glory of God

Romans 5:1 Therefore, since we have been justified by faith, we have peace with God through our Lord Jesus Christ,

Romans 6:23 For the wages of sin is death, but the gift of God is eternal life through Jesus Christ our Lord.

1 Corinthians 15:50-57 Now this I say, brothers, that flesh and blood cannot inherit the kingdom of God, nor does corruption inherit incorruption. Listen, I tell you a mystery: We shall not all sleep, but we shall all be changed. In a moment, in the twinkling of an eye, at the last trumpet, for the trumpet will sound, the dead will be raised incorruptible, and we shall be changed. For this corruptible will put on incorruption, and this mortal will put on immortality. When this corruptible will have put on incorruption, and this mortal will have put on immortality, then the saying that is written shall come to pass: "Death is swallowed up in victory.""O death, where is your sting? O grave, where is your victory?"The sting of death is sin, and the strength of sin is the law. But thanks be to God, who gives us the victory through our Lord Jesus Christ!

Colossians 1:14 in whom we have redemption through His blood, the forgiveness of sins.

1 Peter 2:21-24 For to this you were called, because Christ suffered for us, leaving us an example, that you should follow His steps:"He committed no sin, nor was deceit found in His mouth." When He was reviled, He did not revile back; when He suffered, He did not threaten, but He entrusted Himself to Him who judges righteously. He Himself bore our sins in His own body on the tree, that we, being dead to sins, should live unto righteousness. "By His wounds you were healed."

Revelation 20:15 Anyone whose name was not found written in the Book of Life was cast into the lake of fire.

Revelation 21:1 Then I saw "a new heaven and a new earth."For the first heaven and the first earth had passed away, and there was no more sea.

Revelation 21:4 'God shall wipe away all tears from their eyes. There shall be no more death. 'Neither shall there be any more sorrow nor crying nor pain, for the former things have passed away."

Made in the USA
Middletown, DE
27 November 2022

15788195R00090